Investment Appraisal for
Shareholder Value

FINANCIAL TIMES
Prentice Hall

In an increasingly competitive world, it is quality
of thinking that gives an edge – an idea that opens new
doors, a technique that solves a problem, or an insight
that simply helps make sense of it all.

We work with leading authors in the fields of
management and finance to bring cutting-edge thinking
and best learning practice to a global market.

Under a range of leading imprints, including
Financial Times Prentice Hall, we create world-class
print publications and electronic products giving readers
knowledge and understanding which can then be
applied, whether studying or at work.

To find out more about our business and professional
products, you can visit us at www.business-minds.com

For other Pearson Education publications, visit
www.pearsoned-ema.com

Pearson
Education

Investment Appraisal for Shareholder Value

IAN HIRST

An imprint of Pearson Education

London ■ New York ■ San Francisco ■ Toronto ■ Sydney ■ Tokyo ■ Singapore
Hong Kong ■ Cape Town ■ Madrid ■ Paris ■ Milan ■ Munich ■ Amsterdam

PEARSON EDUCATION LIMITED

Head Office:
Edinburgh Gate
Harlow CM20 2JE
Tel: +44 (0)1279 623623
Fax: +44 (0)1279 431059

London Office:
128 Long Acre
London WC2E 9AN
Tel: +44 (0)20 7447 2000
Fax: +44 (0)20 7240 5771
Website: www.briefingzone.com

First published in Great Britain in 2001

© Pearson Education Limited 2001

The right of Ian Hirst to be identified as author
of this work has been asserted by him in accordance
with the Copyright, Designs and Patents Act 1988.

ISBN 0 273 64220 0

British Library Cataloguing in Publication Data
A CIP catalogue record for this book can be obtained from the British Library.

10 9 8 7 6 5 4 3 2 1

Typeset by Boyd Elliott Typesetting
Printed and bound in Great Britain

The Publishers' policy is to use paper manufactured from sustainable forests.

About the author

Ian Hirst is Professor of Finance at Heriot-Watt University in Edinburgh. He has an MA degree from Oxford University, an MBA from Cornell, and a PhD from the University of Chicago. He has teaching experience at universities in the UK, the US and Australia.

Professor Hirst has considerable experience in teaching project appraisal on MBA programmes to students working as managers in a wide variety of industries. By setting coursework assignments that involved applying modern appraisal methods to current corporate projects, Professor Hirst has learned a great deal about the practical problems of implementing appraisal techniques. The emphases in this briefing on the problems of identifying relevant cash flows, and the importance of including the broader implications of accepting a project (even if they are hard to quantify), are partly a result of this experience.

Professor Hirst is the author of several texts and academic journal articles on project appraisal and other finance topics, including a monograph on 'Business Investment Decisions'. He teaches a CIMA Mastercourse on Capital Investment Appraisal, and has advised leading companies on their appraisal methods and procedures.

The author can be contacted at:

Division of Accountancy and Finance
Heriot-Watt University
Edinburgh EH14 4AT

Contents

Objectives and introduction

INTRODUCTION

The intention of this briefing is to show how current techniques of project appraisal can be used to make value-enhancing investment decisions. It is targeted at financial analysts and others directly involved in making investment decisions. It covers techniques that can be employed – and that are being employed – successfully within major UK companies and internationally. It will explain the procedures and documentation needed to put the techniques into practice.

Using this briefing will enable companies to make better decisions – where 'better' is measured by increases in value for the company shareholders. It is, of course, a standard and rational policy for shareholders to share their increases in wealth, through various mechanisms, with the management team responsible. There should be something in this briefing, gentle reader, for you.

PROJECTS

Projects come in many different forms. Textbooks tend to use examples along the lines of 'company X is considering buying a new machine tool for manufacturing widgets…'. In today's service-based economy, such cases are less typical.

A project is any proposal that involves choosing between the currently foreseen pattern of future corporate cash flows (the 'base case') with another pattern. This includes:

- changing a supply system
- changing a distribution system
- changing credit policy for customers
- changing product warranty
- entering a new market
- developing a new product
- insourcing versus outsourcing a corporate activity
- buying versus making a component
- running a marketing campaign
- acquiring an existing business
- leasing versus buying new equipment
- buying/leasing/renting corporate premises
- updating corporate IT network.

Almost all business decisions with long-term financial consequences can and should be formally appraised.

Common misconceptions

Three common misconceptions about projects are outlined below.

Misconception 1

Projects are linked to physical assets. Projects and assets are quite different things. An *asset* lasts until it rusts, corrodes, becomes unreliable or obsolete. A *project* is an economic opportunity that lasts until the business environment changes. It is rare that the life of an asset and the life of a project will exactly coincide. It is the project, not the asset, which needs to be appraised.

Case study 1.1

At Anonymous plc, the chief executive was concerned about the continuing high level of expenditure on new computers and related equipment. 'I've never seen a new piece of kit come through the door that wasn't out again within five years because you have given me some complicated story about how it needs to be replaced by something bigger or better or faster. Very well then. All new IT projects in this company have to be justified over a life of no more than five years'.

The logic here is wrong. The *project* of adapting Anonymous (and many other companies) to new technology will be a very long-term project that is essential for corporate survival. In the process, the company will go though many items of equipment in just the same way that a cricket team will go though a lot of cricket balls. There is no reason to limit the life of a project to the life of an item of equipment that it uses.

Misconception 2

The criteria for including an item in a project appraisal is the same as the criteria for entering an item in company accounts – except that company accounts look to the past and project appraisal looks to the future.

No. The whole approach is different in the two cases. Company accounting is based on principles that include prudence, conservatism, objective verifiability, and a high degree of certainty. In the right context, these are splendid virtues but project appraisal is not the right context. Any attempt to confine project appraisal to cash flows that are safe is doomed to fail. Major projects are usually risky. Look at some of the stellar investment decisions in the UK in recent years, for example BSkyB's decision to buy Premier League football rights; Racal's decision to move into mobile phones; Dixon's decision to set up Freeserve. Each of these investments required an imaginative estimation of how a new market might develop.

To change the analogy, a project is not like a criminal trial, where the verdict has to be proved 'beyond reasonable doubt'. It is more like a civil dispute, to be decided 'on the balance of the evidence'. Anyone working in project appraisal will have to get used to estimates that are based on informed (and perhaps inspired) judgement as well as hard data.

Misconception 3

A lot of projects can't be appraised. This misconception comes in three flavours.

First, that the company has 'no choice' but to invest to meet new health regulations/match competitors' product specifications, etc. No choice – and therefore no opportunity for appraisal – is very rare. One alternative to meeting health regulations is to close down the offending operation and use an external source (or an in-company source located in another jurisdiction). One of the ways in which investment enthusiasts push their projects through with few questions asked is to claim there is 'no alternative'. Be suspicious of this argument. Some companies require that at least two alternatives are presented alongside every investment proposal, and this is a good discipline.

Second, that the project cannot be appraised in a quantitative way because no relevant data are available. This, again, is an argument to be viewed with suspicion. Coming up with some sort of numerical appraisal should be viewed as a challenge – and one that a good financial analyst can usually win.

Case study 1.2

A company is discussing redecorating the staff canteen. MBA students are often willing to class this as an unappraisable project, and to assume that management will have to make a subjective judgement. The very idea of appraising a refurbishment scheme can often raise a laugh in the classroom.

Think again! Suppose a £15,000 investment is expected to last five years. We know how many meals are eaten in the canteen each year. It will be a simple calculation (covered later in this briefing) to work out the extra cost per meal. Put up an illustration of the new scheme and take an office poll, asking 'Would it be worth an extra Xp to you to eat a meal in these new surroundings?' Better still, show several different refurbishment schemes with different prices and ask which staff would prefer. Since staff like to be consulted, this might even have a positive effect on morale.

Third, that the project is 'strategic' – it is large and central to the company's future – and so the mundane disciplines of appraisal can be overridden. This is a common argument but, looked at closely, it is a very strange one. The project is being classed as 'too important' to be subject to formal analysis.

Strategic projects do have special characteristics. They position the company to take advantage of emerging trends in the marketplace. The value of this sort of 'positioning' is certainly hard to calculate, but this does not imply that the job is not worth doing. Strategic decisions are often linked to the acquisition of 'real options' – the opportunity to make future investments in reaction to developments in demand, fashion or technology. Options are not easy to value, but we have some useful approaches which will be discussed in more detail later.

SHAREHOLDER VALUE

Whether we like it or not, the financial system in the UK and other developed countries requires that managers should focus their efforts single-mindedly on increasing the wealth of their shareholders. Managers who are reluctant to embrace this objective are replaced by those who are more amenable.

An increase in shareholder wealth can be difficult to define when a company goes through financial changes which involve splitting or combining shares. Leaving these cases aside, however, increasing shareholder wealth simply means getting the share price up.

Share price movements will, of course, depend on many factors in addition to investment decisions. The whole market may rise or fall; other company projects may turn for better or for worse. However, leaving all these other factors aside, a good project is one that will make the share price go up and a bad project will make it go down.

Let's look more closely at the relationship between projects and the share price.

Is it true that share prices usually respond positively to company investments? Isn't the stock market short-termist, with a preference for high dividends rather than putting cash into long-term projects?

'Yes' to the first question. 'No' to the second. While there are many studies which show that, on average, when a company announces a new investment the share price goes up, there are also exceptions to this. One famous study showed that, for US oil companies in the early 1980s, share prices fell when new exploration programmes were announced. This was a time when the prices of oil and of oil shares were low. It was cheaper to buy oil reserves by taking over an oil company than by drilling for them. Not surprisingly, the stock market punished companies which made the wrong, inefficient choice.

However, most investment projects are not perverse in this way and the market reacts positively when they are announced.

Much is written about the short-termism of the stock market – most of it completely unjustified by hard evidence. At the time of writing, the dividend yield on the FTSE 100 is 2.25 per cent; in the information technology sector it is 0.46 per cent. This hardly squares with the assertion that investors demand quick cash returns. The evidence suggests that, so long as they are convinced that the long-term prospects are good, investors are very willing to support company investment programmes.

When will the share price react to investment decisions?

The stock market responds to new, unexpected information. Only surprises will make the share price move suddenly.

People are sometimes puzzled by stock market reactions. In 1997, Laura Ashley announced profits up by 73 per cent and the share price fell sharply on the same day. Why? Presumably the stock market consensus had been anticipating an even bigger profit increase.

So we will not see a simple, simultaneous relationship between good investment decisions and share price rises. The stock market will have already formed a view of a company's likely investment programme and its profitability. It is only when an announcement changes the market expectations that the share price will be affected.

Even if an investment decision will create shareholder value, the share price may not rise when it is announced. The share price may even go the wrong way if the market had been anticipating something better.

So, does managing for shareholder value mean looking for the approval of fund managers and other major investors before making decisions? Surely they do not understand the business as well as management? Investors – whether they are professional fund mangers or private individuals – do not want to run the company and do not want to get involved in the detail of investment decisions. They recognise that they are less well informed than management and they expect management to take the lead in making investment decisions.

However, they do expect management to explain and to justify the decisions they make. As long as management–investor communication is good, and investors find management presentations credible, then the gap between shareholder value assessed by in-company financial analysis and shareholder value as measured on the stock market will be small. Sometimes, however, the gap will be large. This will be an anomalous situation, in which management's appraisal of value differs from the market's. It should not last for long; one side or the other will be proved right. Managers' jobs are in danger if *they* have made the error.

Management should be prepared to back their own best judgement even if this conflicts with conventional or market wisdom. This is the job that they have been hired to do. Managing for shareholder value does not mean that managers must constantly look to the investment community for approval of every decision that they make. It does mean that they should be in constant communication with investors to ensure that, as far as possible, investors share management's perception of the future. A focus on shareholder value includes a focus on communication with shareholders.

Case study 1.3

Barrie Stephens, chief executive of Siebe, decided to bid for a US company, Foxboro Controls. Siebe was already in the controls business, and it saw the potential for high margins and fast growth. Foxboro was in trouble. It had spent a lot of money developing new technology and the fruits had not yet appeared on the bottom line. Siebe knew that the new technology had excellent prospects. The investment community in London was aware of a long succession of ill-judged takeovers by UK companies in America and was not sanguine about the prospects for this one.

When Siebe announced the takeover, its share price fell sharply – a reaction that Barrie Stephens could have predicted. Does this mean that his decision violated the principle of maximising shareholder wealth?

No, Siebe's management were employing their own judgement in the pursuit of shareholder wealth – and they would be remiss if they did *not* use their own judgement. If shareholders lose confidence in their judgement, then it is up to the shareholder body (and possibly the independent directors) to remove them.

This story has a happy ending – Foxboro turned out to be a brilliant acquisition. But the point is a general one. The question of whether an investment is value creating or not does not turn on one day's stock market reaction. However, Siebe's management should certainly be aware of investors' concerns, and should work actively to convince the market that, despite past precedents, this US acquisition was a good buy.

FINDING PROJECTS

Good projects are the raw material from which shareholder value is created. If they were easy to find, every manager could look like a genius. Unfortunately, there is intense competition between companies for good projects, and competition drives project costs up (think of the fees paid to 'bankable' stars by movie companies) and project revenues down. In fact, in a world of perfect competition, there would be no good projects that could add to shareholder wealth.

Projects are to be found in the cracks, crevices and other imperfections of the marketplace. Your company is only going to be able to find good projects by exploiting some competitive advantage that it possesses. To create the greatest possible shareholder value, it must exploit these advantages to the maximum.

A key source of competitive advantage for companies is their specialist knowledge of the markets within which they operate. A briefing such as this – designed for a wide range of different companies and industries – cannot offer specific project ideas. But there are several points to keep in mind when hunting for new investment ideas.

Are managers encouraged to generate ideas?

It is unlikely that all the good ideas will come from the boardroom. People are at their most creative and most in touch with social and technical developments in their 20s and 30s. The average age of many boards is over 50. Companies therefore need to search throughout their organisations for new investment ideas. Most divisional managers are very aware of their obligation to keep their financial record in line with the company plan. Have they been made equally aware of their obligation to generate new cost-saving and business growth ideas? Would these ideas get a full and fair hearing at the top? Is there an incentive system in place that rewards them and their staff for doing this? Is 'asking for more money' seen as a corporate crime?

Case study 1.4

In the 1970s and 1980s, Hanson and BTR were two of the stars of the London stock market. They were both huge 'diversified industrials' which had grown through making very large numbers of acquisitions. At its peak, BTR contained 1,500 different operating units. In the 1990s both these companies' share prices went into decline. Hanson broke itself up; BTR made major disposals and then disappeared through a merger. What had gone wrong?

Both these companies had a culture of 'making the numbers' – generating high earnings each year to impress the city. They cut operating costs and inessential items such as research budgets. They raised prices. They had little interest in growing their businesses – indeed, management at the top level knew little about the underlying technologies on which their businesses were based. Notoriously, Hanson's battery business, starved of R&D money, missed the technology switch to long-life batteries, and surrendered a strong market position.

One of the lessons of this debacle is that a company which is not focused on hunting for good investment opportunities is a company which is not genuinely focused on shareholder value.

Case study 1.5

In recent years the giant UK brewers have been repositioning themselves as leisure companies and building up portfolios of leisure brands. It is notable that they have acquired many of their new brands at high prices (David Lloyd Leisure, which was acquired by

Whitbread is a good example) rather than growing them in-house. Could more vigorous backing for internally generated investment ideas have created more wealth for shareholders? To an outsider, it certainly looks that way.

Do we really have a competitive advantage in making this investment?

Stock market cynics have defined a mine as a hole in the ground with a liar at the top. Projects start as numbers on a spreadsheet with a 'project champion' in front of them. The numbers always look good. How can the project reviewers separate the wheat from the chaff?

One approach for new-venture projects is to ask what advantage the company has over rivals in carrying it out. No competitive advantage means little opportunity for adding shareholder value.

Case study 1.6

The early years in the PC business were a gold rush. A comparison between the price at which PCs were being sold and the cost of the components made the business look irresistibly attractive. There would be start-up costs for case design, marketing and distribution but thereafter it would be all good news. Dozens of companies moved into the industry.

Before long, they were nearly all out again with their fingers badly burned. PC prices fell rapidly. The profit forecasts had been a mirage, based on temporary imbalances in a fast-evolving market. It could surely always have been foreseen that competitive advantage in assembling and marketing PCs would go to companies with economies of scale linked to strong distribution and branding.

What is the stock market telling us?

An immediate positive response from the stock market is not necessarily the hallmark of a good investment, as explained above. But this does not mean that the opinion of the market is valueless. Share prices give a general guide whether the market thinks that a company has a lot of good investment opportunities. The technique involves the calculation of present value of growth opportunities (PVGO).

PVGO calculation

The market value of companies can be divided into two parts. The first is the value of existing operations. The second is the value of the opportunities to develop profitable new operations in the future.

A simple way to measure the value of existing operations is to assume that the current level of profit will continue indefinitely into the future. The value of growth opportunities is the residual element of company value after existing operations have been subtracted.

Consider two UK companies – Glaxo Wellcome (a pharmaceuticals company) and Imperial Tobacco. Information on these two companies is given below.

Table 1.1 Market information: Glaxo Wellcome and Imperial Tobacco

	Glaxo Wellcome	Imperial Tobacco
Market cap	£63,600m	£ 3,400m
Forecast earnings	£2,030m	£270m
Required return	12.5%	9.9%
Value of existing operations	£16,240m	£2,730m
Value of growth opportunities	£47,360m	£670m
% of market value derived from growth opportunities	75%	20%

The method of estimating required returns is covered later in this briefing. Since the forecast earnings are assumed to continue in perpetuity generated by existing operations, the present value of this perpetuity is found by dividing current earnings by the required return.

These simple calculations hold a lesson for management of these two companies. The stock market does not believe that Imperial Tobacco has big, valuable investment opportunities. Imperial might have an opportunity to prove the investment community wrong. If it does find such an opportunity it should certainly take it. But, in most cases, the stock market view will be a realistic one, and Imperial's management should be quite prepared to pay out generous dividends or to carry out share buybacks rather than use their cash to grow the business.

The message for Glaxo Wellcome is quite the opposite. Here management will severely disappoint the market if they fail to find major investment opportunities. If Glaxo's management were to announce a share buyback, the share price would be likely to fall sharply. It would look as though they had failed to find enough good projects to use their available cash.

The point of these PVGO calculations is not that management should be ruled by the stock market's view, but that the market's view is worth taking into account and should not be ignored.

Can we get finance?

If you have a good project, it is highly likely that you will obtain finance for it. Even if internal funds are insufficient, a whole range of financial markets exists to match investors with good projects.

It is wrong to think that the firm's pool of capital is fixed in size and that the investment programme has to be chopped or stretched to fit. There should be no 'investment budget'.

The idea that investment projects should be chosen to create value for shareholders is in direct conflict with any scheme to set an investment budget for the company (or for its component divisions). The right amount to spend each year will emerge as investment proposals pass or fail the appraisal process. It cannot be set far in advance as a percentage of sales or by any other formula. Financial markets are sufficiently flexible (at least for large companies) that funds can be found when there is a good use for them. Investment budgets are generally a sign the management has abdicated its responsibilities and taken the easy option as a way of avoiding internal arguments.

THE ORGANISATION OF THIS BRIEFING

Most readers will have a basic knowledge of Net Present Value (NPV) and Cost of Capital. Chapter 2 *The basic logic of present value* will review this material.

The next two chapters look at the problems involved in putting the basic principles into practice. Chapter 3 looks at *Defining relevant cash flows*, and Chapter 4 discusses *Risk-adjusted returns*.

Chapter 5 *NPV Techniques* looks at two methods of NPV calculation. The first, Weighted Average Cost of Capital (WACC) is a simple but imprecise method which is very widely used, especially for projects that are modest in size and typical of the company's activities. It is well suited to a decentralised appraisal process. The alternative method, Adjusted Present Value (APV) is more complex but more accurate and can include project-specific financing packages in the analysis.

The problems of project appraisal are very largely associated with risk. Chapter 6 *Risk analysis* looks at several ways in which the appraisal can be modified to take the range of possible outcomes into account. It covers:

- Sensitivity Analysis

- Monte Carlo Simulation

- real options analysis.

Chapter 7 *Specialised appraisal methods* looks at three situations for which specialised appraisal methods are available:

- cross-border investments

- asset replacement and investment timing

- lease analysis.

Chapter 8 gives a brief summary and, as an aid to the management of the appraisal process, provides an example of an appropriate standard set of information for investment appropriation requests.

The basic logic of present value

INTRODUCTION

This chapter explains the fundamental ideas on which investment appraisal is based and covers:

- the time value of money and interest calculations
- appraisal measures – Net Present Value (NPV), Internal Rate of Return (IRR), Payback, Economic Profit
- the cost of capital – equity cost related to risk using the Capital Asset Pricing Model (CAPM); debt cost adjusted for tax; and the weighted average cost of a financial mix.

The problems of applying these ideas in the complex reality of the business environment are discussed in later chapters. Readers already familiar with these basic ideas can move directly to Chapter 3.

THE TIME VALUE OF MONEY

Investors expect their money to grow. Capital is a useful factor of production. It can claim a return, just as workers can claim a return for their labour. The return is usually expressed as an annual rate.

Investors who are highly risk-averse can choose a rate of return which is certain. This is the risk-free rate of interest. If this rate is 8 per cent (0.08) then an investor's savings will grow as follows:

Year 0	Year 1	Year 2	Year 3	Year 4	Year 5
100	$100(1+0.08)$	$100(1+0.08)^2$	$100(1+0.08)^3$	$100(1+08)^4$	$100(1+0.08)^5$
	$=108.00$	$=116.64$	$=125.97$	$=136.05$	$=146.93$

In general, if the interest rate is R, the growth of the savings will be:

100	$100(1+R)$	$100(1+R)^2$	$100(1+R)^3$	$100(1+R)^4$	$100(1+R)^5$

The same formula applies to fractions of years. After 2 years and 9 months ($9/12 = 0.75$ of a year), the savings would have grown to $100\,(1+R)^{2.75}$, or, at 8%:

$$100(1.08)^{2.75} = 123.57$$

All these amounts of money (£100 today; £136.05 after 4 years; £123.57 after 2.75 years) are *exchangeable for each other*. They have equal value, and the standard way of measuring the value is in terms of year 0 value, generally termed *present value*.

This exchangeability goes both ways. If the interest rate is 8 per cent, an individual can deposit £100 in a bank today and take out £125.97 in three years. Equally, he can borrow £100 today and promise to repay £125.97 in three years' time (assuming he can persuade the bank his promise is good). We are clearly simplifying here. Borrowing rates and lending rates are not identical and the difference between them is highly significant for banks and other financial intermediaries. But the differences are small fractions of 1 per cent for most substantial businesses and we shall ignore them. At 8 per cent, £100 has a future value of £116.94 in two years; a future amount of £100 has a present value of $100/(1.08)^2 = £85.73$.

The present value of any future amount of cash is measured by its exchange value in terms of current money. This amount calculated using an interest rate. The present value is *not* the sum of money which would buy today what the future amount would buy when it arrives. A present value is *not* a 'purchasing power equivalent'. It is an equivalent in market value.

VALUING A STREAM OF CASH FLOWS

Any project, say to create a new video game, will generate a sequence of cash flows. An aggregate present value can be calculated from these. If the cash flows are:

Year 1	Year 2	Year 3	Year 4	Year 5
100	250	350	400	200

The total present value at an interest rate of 11 per cent would be:

$$\frac{100}{1.11} + \frac{250}{(1.11)^2} + \frac{350}{(1.11)^3} + \frac{400}{(1.11)^4} + \frac{200}{(1.11)^5}$$

$$= 90.09 + 202.91 + 255.92 + 263.49 + 118.69 = 931.10$$

The term 'Net Present Value' refers to the present value of the cash flows from a project after the initial investment to set it up has been subtracted. If the video game cash flows above could be obtained by spending £800 in year 0, then the NPV of the whole project would be:

$$-800 + 931.10 = 131.10$$

The outflows to set up the project are treated in exactly the same way as the subsequent inflows. The 800 has not been discounted because it takes place in Year 0.

Months and years

As in most texts, this briefing uses a year as the standard period of time; this simplifies the examples. Most companies make their cash forecasts on a monthly basis. This is no problem for present value calculations.

If the interest rate is 1 per cent per month, the rate of growth over a year is calculated as follows:

$$\text{Since } (1.01)^{12} = 1.1268, \text{ the annual rate is } 12.68\%.$$

Conversely, if the annual rate was 12 per cent, the monthly rate would be calculated as follows:

$$(1 + r)^{12} = 1.12$$
$$1 + r = 1.0095 \qquad r = 0.0095$$

If the annual interest rate was 12 per cent, and we wanted to discount the following monthly cash flows back to present value (Month 0), we would calculate:

	Month 0	Month 1	Month 2	Month 3	Month 4
Cash flow		100	150	200	150
Cash flows converted to present value		$\dfrac{100}{1.0095}$ $= 99.06$	$\dfrac{150}{(1.0095)^2}$ $= 14.19$	$\dfrac{200}{(1.0095)^3}$ $= 194.41$	$\dfrac{150}{(1.0095)^4}$ $= 144.43$
Total present value	585.09				

THE INTERPRETATION OF NET PRESENT VALUE

Converting all the cash flows from a project into their present value equivalents and then adding them up gives a direct measure of what a project is worth. If this NPV is negative, then the project is worthless and should be abandoned. If the NPV is positive, it should be accepted.

Suppose that you are a house-building company and you have just received planning permission for land on which you have an option. *The NPV of the cash flows from developing the land measures what the project is worth.* It therefore represents the minimum price at which you would be willing to sell the project (by selling the option) to another company. Assume that:

- the stock market does not know about the project in advance, so value relating to the project is not in the share price already
- tax payable is accurately incorporated in the analysis
- the stock market understands the full consequences of the project as soon as it is announced.

The NPV measures how much the stock market value of the company will rise when the project is announced. NPV is therefore directly linked to stock market value. Stock market value is maximised when projects are accepted or rejected on the basis of their NPV.

OTHER APPRAISAL METHODS

NPV is one of several appraisal numbers that can be calculated.

Payback period

The *payback period* is the number of years until the original outlay has been recovered. With the video game cash flows shown below, the payback period is 3.25 years. All of the cash flows from the first three years, plus a quarter of the cash flow in year 4, are needed to match the initial outlay of 800.

Year 0	Year 1	Year 2	Year 3	Year 4	Year 5
−800	+100	+250	+350	+400	+200

Some companies set a minimum payback period for their projects, say three years. This approach makes no sense.

- The minimum payback period is generally chosen quite arbitrarily.
- The calculation ignores the time value of money. Simply adding together cash flows from different years is as unhelpful as adding together a number of euros and a number of dollars.
- The calculation ignores the cash flows beyond the payback period; yet these cash flows are vital components of project value. Payback fails to indicate whether a project will create shareholder value.

Is payback useful as a tie-breaker?

If you are choosing between two projects with the same NPV, would you choose the one with the quicker payback? The answer is 'No', since the payback number adds no useful information here. There is no reason to have a bias towards short-lived projects. Companies are in business to create value (measured by NPV), and value created by long-term projects is every bit as good as value created by short-term ones.

Discounted payback

It is also possible to calculate *discounted payback*. Using the present values at 11 per cent which were calculated above, the discounted cash flows are:

Year 0	Year 1	Year 2	Year 3	Year 4	Year 5
−800	90.09	202.91	255.92	263.49	118.9

Using these numbers the discounted payback for the video game project is 3.95 years. If we assume that all the cash flows after the initial investment stage are positive (and often they are not), then discounted payback does have one advantage. If a discounted payback period can be calculated, then there is a positive NPV. However, the calculation adds no useful information to the NPV number.

Internal Rate of Return

Another common measure of project attractiveness is the Internal Rate of Return (IRR). This approach looks at the project as if it were a bank – you deposit money today and you can draw money out later. If a sign in a bank's window says 'Deposit £5,000 today and we will give you back £8,000 in 5 years' time', savers would immediately ask 'What rate of return does that give me?' The answer is 9.8 per cent, because the present value of £8,000 at this rate just matches the £5,000 initial investment.

$$\frac{8,000}{(1.098)^5} - 5,000 = 0$$

We can do the same for the video game cash flow. Since

$$-800 + \frac{100}{1.166} + \frac{250}{(1.166)^2} + \frac{350}{(1.166)^3} + \frac{400}{(1.166)^4} + \frac{200}{(1.166)^5} = 0$$

21

the IRR of the project is 16.6 per cent. If we believe that 11 per cent is the appropriate discount rate, then this project should be accepted. It gives a return on the shareholders' money which exceeds their rate of discount.

How do we solve the equation for IRR? Don't try it with pen, paper and calculator. It is a tedious job. Spreadsheet packages have a special function. For example, in Microsoft's Excel the command is simply

$$= IRR \text{ (cash flows)}$$

The cash flows can be typed into the command, or they can be identified elsewhere on the spreadsheet – for example A1 : A10.

IRR is often used to appraise projects. Although it takes the time value of money into account, it has major weaknesses.

■ IRR appraisal only works when the project has a conventional pattern of cash flows – initial outflows followed by inflows. If the pattern is more complex and there is more than one change of sign in the sequence of cash flows, then there will be more than one IRR. This curious mathematical fact makes IRR unusable in these cases. If a project has 'reverse cash flows' (i.e. inflows followed by outflows, and there are many such projects), then the project is analagous to borrowing money from a bank and a *low* IRR is preferred.

■ IRR cannot be used to rank projects. It does not show which project to choose if there are several good projects which are mutually exclusive. A project with a 50 per cent IRR is not necessarily preferable to one with a 45 per cent IRR. Forty-five per cent might be available on a big, long-term project – and that might be preferable to a 50 per cent return on a small project.

NPV calculations solve both these problems. A positive NPV shows that value is being created for shareholders whatever the pattern of cash flows. And, if a choice has to be made between good projects, the right choice is to pick the individual project, or set of projects, with the highest NPV.

IRR numbers can lead to errors. If a 15 per cent IRR is good, wouldn't 25 per cent be even better? If we refuse to accept any investment with a return of less than 25 per cent won't that show how aggressive we are in pursuit of shareholder value? This approach is nonsense. If your investors can only get 11 per cent elsewhere, then you are not doing them a favour by turning down a chance to earn 15 per cent. Companies that set too high a cut-off for IRR destroy value for their shareholders just as surely as those who set the cut-off too low.

Using forecast profit for investment appraisal

People generally believe that a company's annual profits are the measure of how much wealth has been created for shareholders. This is wrong for several reasons; one is that subjective judgements and arbitrary accounting rules lie behind the numbers.

Another central problem with accounting profits is that they don't make proper allowance for the time value of money. In the simplest possible case, suppose a company takes £100 from investors and turns it into £105 by the end of the year. This will be shown as an accounting profit of £5. But has the company created value for the investors? If they could have earned 8 per cent by depositing their money in a bank, an accurate measure would show that the company has destroyed value for the investors.

Another definition of profit (economic profit) measures what is left over after charges for all factors of production used by the firm, including capital, have been deducted. Let's apply this logic to the video game example. The company has invested £800, so the capital charge in the first year (at 11 per cent) is £88. If the capital investment loses value at the constant rate of 160 per year then the calculations of economic profit are:

	Year 1	Year 2	Year 3	Year 4	Year 5
Cash flow	100.0	250.0	350.0	400.0	200.0
less Capital Charge	88.0	70.4	52.8	35.2	17.6
less fall in Capital Value	160.0	160.0	160.0	160.0	160.0
Economic Profit	−148.0	19.6	137.2	204.8	22.4

If we calculate the present value of this stream of economic profit we get:

$$\frac{-148}{1.11} + \frac{19.6}{(1.11)^2} + \frac{137.2}{(1.11)^3} + \frac{204.8}{(1.11)^4} + \frac{22.4}{(1.11)^5} = 131.10$$

This number is the project's NPV that we calculated earlier.

Projects, therefore, can be appraised on the basis of the profit they will produce but it must be economic profit and not accounting profit. Measures of accounting profit or accounting return on investment are not useful.

The value of the economic profit calculations might also seem to be dubious. After all, the NPV can be calculated more easily without using the concept at all. However, companies are often interested in measuring value creation on a year-by-year basis – perhaps as a basis for rewarding managers – so measurement of annual economic profit for companies and divisions is now quite common. There are well-developed proprietory systems available of which the best known is probably Economic Value Added (EVA).

WHY IS NPV UNLOVED?

In real corporate life, NPV is not the runaway winner in the investment appraisal stakes that it deserves to be. A lot of companies use it, but usually alongside other approaches.

Does NPV seem a bit 'greedy' in revealing the size of the loot to be gained? Will the staff ask 'If you are making this much out of the project, how come you can't give us a bigger pay rise?' Is it a problem that NPV fails to give any sense of proportion? An NPV of £1million gained by investing £5million, is just as attractive as an NPV of £1million gained by investing £50million – but, in the second case, it might take only a small percentage change in the cash flows to wipe out, or to double, the NPV. Sensitivity analysis, which looks at this type of issue, is covered later in this briefing, but a correctly calculated NPV number has already taken risk into account, as we shall see later, through the discount rate.

COST OF CAPITAL

An NPV calculation requires the selection of a discount rate. The rate is often called the 'cost of capital'. The cost of capital for a project is an opportunity cost. It is also risk-related. It is the rate of return that investors could have earned if they had invested their money elsewhere in a company or project offering the same level of risk. The return expected by investors is the funding cost to the company – these terms describe the same concept viewed from different sides.

Companies will generally acquire capital from savers via several different routes. For example, they may borrow from banks or issue long-term bonds, or they may sell shares that will be quoted on the stock market. There are more exotic possibilities such as convertible bonds. Each of these sources of funds will have a different cost, and the costs will vary for two significant reasons. In addition to the underlying base cost of funds, there will be:

- cost linked to the level risk imposed on a class of capital
- a reduction in cost linked to any tax breaks awarded a class of capital.

These are major factors. Bank finance may cost a little more because a bank is an intermediary between the saver and the company, and it has to charge for its services. It may be that long-term bonds can only be sold with legal clauses that restrict the issuing companies' future decisions and this is another form of cost. These issues will be part of the technical complexity of a finance director's job but they are secondary in comparison with *risk* and *tax*, the big drivers behind cost of capital.

The base cost of capital

This is the risk-free interest rate. Since the Government is the least risky borrower around, the base cost is measured as the return available on Government debt. In the UK the generally accepted measure is the return on three-month Treasury Bills, a rate which is published daily in the financial press.

The cost of risk

The fact that risk is an intangible concept does not prevent the financial markets from pricing risk in just the same way that wheat and coal are priced. Any class of capital carries a level of risk as well as an expected return. Normally, almost all the risk is born by the equity capital. The quantity of risk associated with a particular share can be measured, and the cost of share capital to a company is directly related to the number of units of risk (appropriately measured) that the shareholders are being asked to take, just as the cost of refuse collection from a factory will be directly related to the number of truckloads of refuse that have to be carried away. By the natural working of the market price, the price per unit of risk will be a standard level throughout the economy. We therefore need to identify:

- the amount of risk associated with particular equity ownership rights
- the 'price' (additional return) associated with each unit of risk.

Measuring risk

Risk perceived inside a company tends to be the risk of losing customers, of rises in raw material prices, of adverse regulatory decisions, etc. However, the investor is not impacted by these things directly. Shareholders perceive risk in terms of movements in the value of their shares. This is usually measured as the standard deviation of returns over the recent past. There are several sources of this information, including the Risk Measurement Service of the London Business School. There are also commercial (non-academic) information providers. Figure

2.1 shows the historic standard deviation of return for a small sample of major UK companies.

Fig. 2.1 Historic standard deviation of return for UK companies

Company	Overall risk (standard deviation %)	ß	Specific risk (standard deviation %)
BAA	26	0.88	24
British Airways	30	1.47	25
Land Securities	21	0.54	20
Courtaulds Textiles	41	0.91	40
Diageo	22	1.01	19
Boots	21	0.64	20
Lloyds TSB	26	1.41	20

Source: LBS Risk Measurement Service Jan–March 2000

However, the expected return on shares is not directly related to this standard deviation. Rational investors do not invest in a single share; they buy a portfolio of shares and by doing so they diversify their risk. The risk of an individual share can be divided into two distinct components, and these components interact in very different ways when a number of shares are held together in a portfolio. The two types of risk are:

- market-related risk
- specific risk.

Market-related risk (or systematic risk)

All shares tend to respond to general movements in the level of the stock market but shares differ in their sensitivity to such movements. The measure of a share's sensitivity is the beta-coefficient (β) of the share.

For share x, β_x measures the extra percentage return on share x normally associated with an extra 1 per cent return on the stock market index. Notice that the average β of all the shares in the market is going to be one because if the stock market index goes up 1 per cent this must mean that shares, on average, have risen 1 per cent. But the βs of individual shares will vary widely. Many shares will have βs substantially above 1 and many will have βs substantially below.

The difference between the two types of company was well illustrated in the stock market crash of October 1987. The market fell by 30 per cent over two days, although not all shares fell in equal proportions.

The share that fell most was Britannia Arrow, a fund management company. Britannia Arrow ran unit trusts which it marketed to retail investors. The fall in the market was doubly bad news because:

■ the company's revenue was a percentage of the value of its funds

■ a crash is likely to deter retail investors.

Britannia Arrow shares performed badly when the market fell. They had done exceptionally well in the earlier part of 1987 when the market had risen strongly. They are a good example of a high β share.

The share that fell the least in the crash was Safeway, the food retailer. If the crash was signalling an economic downturn, people would continue to buy baked beans. They might even buy more beans than they had originally intended. Safeway shares fell less in the crash, and had risen less in the previous boom, than the market average. Safeway was a low β share.

The β of a share is certainly linked, as these examples show, to the nature of the company's business. It is also influenced by a company's financial structure. If a company uses a lot of debt in its capital structure, then the operating risks of the business are loaded onto a restricted volume of risk capital, and the risk level of the shares can be high even though the underlying business is comparatively low risk. This has occurred in the case of many utility companies in the UK. When they were originally privatised they were almost debt-free and, as very stable businesses, their βs were low. A decade or so later they had transformed their finances, they had taken on a lot of debt and their βs were much higher. Examples of β coefficients are shown in Figure 2.1.

Specific risk (or unsystematic risk)

Share price volatility that is not related to general movements in the market is called specific risk. Shares go up or down because a contract has been won, a new drug has been approved, a chief executive has resigned, etc. These are single company events and every company has a level of specific risk (measured as a standard deviation) caused by them. Values of specific risk for a sample of companies are also shown in Figure 2.1.

The effects of diversification

When the specific risks from a number of different companies are put together in a portfolio, they melt away. The mathematics of diversification show that when investors spread their wealth evenly over 30 or so different shares, the level of specific risk that remains is very small. To put this another way, a portfolio of 30 or more shares will tend to move very closely with the stock market as a whole.

Investors diversify and specific risk disappears. The only category of risk that impacts on investors, and for which they need to be compensated by extra return, is market-related risk measured by β.

This brilliant, counter-intuitive insight is called the Capital Asset Pricing Model. The model is shown graphically in Figure 2.2.

Fig. 2.2 Capital asset pricing model

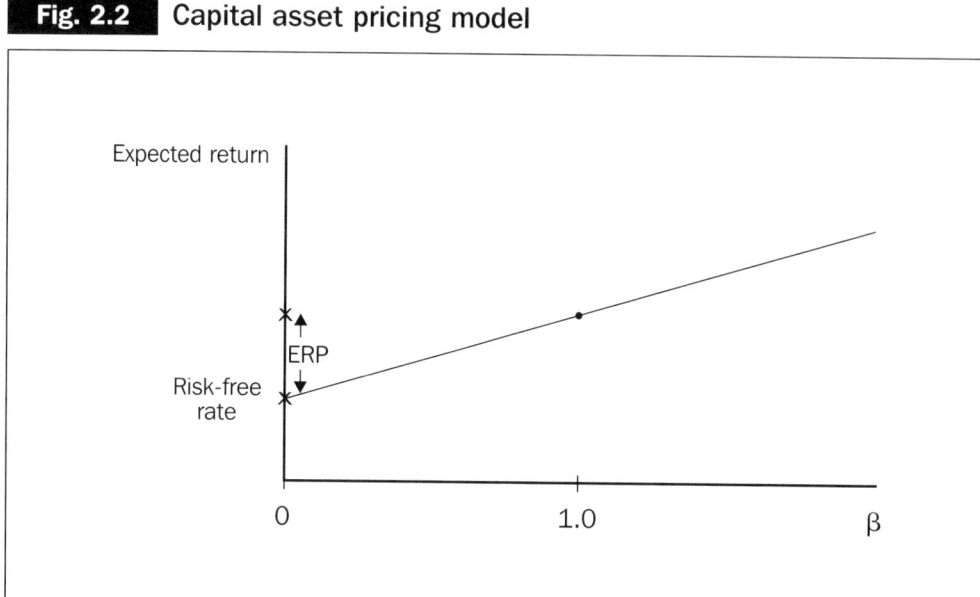

Figure 2.2 shows that the cost of risk capital to any company x is a basic 'risk-free' cost and an additional risk-related premium of $K\beta$, where K is a constant which applies equally to all shares in the marketplace. K is often termed the 'equity risk premium' (ERP). It is the return that an investor can expect if he buys a portfolio of shares that replicates the whole market (an index-tracker fund is an example of such a portfolio, it has $\beta = 1$) *less* the basic return available from a risk-free investment (e.g. Treasury Bills).

The evidence of the past 80 years in the UK is that K has averaged 6.5 per cent. We can use this rate to illustrate a CAPM calculation. In early 2000 the Treasury Bill rate was 5.8%. So for Tesco ($\beta = 1.05$) the cost of equity capital would be:

$$5.8\% + (6.50\% \times 1.05) = 12.6\%$$

The value of the equity risk premium is a highly controversial issue. But the CAPM has been a very valuable advance, which has shown how the cost of funds are linked to the level of risk that they carry.

TAX SUBSIDIES

It is not immediately obvious why public policy should give tax advantages to one type of finance rather than another. It is even less clear why governments would want to discriminate in favour of property companies and against hi-tech start-ups. This is the case in most developed economies. Corporate tax is charged on profits remaining after interest payments have been deducted. Property companies can offer good security for loans; they take on substantial debts and gain a large 'tax shelter' as a result. Start-ups are not creditworthy to the same extent and their profits cannot be sheltered.

Suppose a company using capital of £200 is choosing between all equity finance and a 50/50 split between debt and equity. Its earnings before interest and tax (EBIT) will be £50, and the corporate tax rate is 40 per cent. The cost of debt is 10 per cent. How much will shareholders get in each case?

	All-equity Finance	50% Debt/50% Equity
EBIT	50	50
Interest	-	10
Taxable income	50	40
Tax at 40%	20	16
Profit for shareholders	30	24

Comparing the two columns shows that paying £10 of interest only costs the shareholders £6. The debt has effectively cost only 6 per cent. The other £4 is generously provided as a subsidy by the Inland Revenue. In general, if the interest rate is I and the corporate tax rate is T, the cost of debt from the shareholders' perspective is $I(1 - T)$. For equity finance, the cost would start at I even before the extra costs for bearing risk are added. Debt therefore has a built-in financial advantage.

THE FINANCING MIX

All equity finance is likely to be tax inefficient. All debt finance is impossible. Lenders will need to see an adequate volume of risk-bearing equity in place before they lend. Most companies and projects will be financed by a debt/equity mixture. The cost of a mixture is simply the weighted average of the two (or more) components.

Cost of capital = (Proportion of debt × cost of debt) + (Proportion of equity × cost of equity).

The difficulties involved in calculating the appropriate proportions are discussed later in this briefing. Notice, however, a paradox. The capital used in a particular project is generally not the capital that is raised when the project is launched. When capital is raised, it needs to be raised in large tranches. The fixed costs of negotiation, paperwork and 'information costs' ensure this. This is particularly true for issuing equity capital. So, although the finance director may have a 'target' debt/equity ratio, at any point in time, the ratio may be some way away from target. At infrequent intervals, major financial restructuring will reset the ratio closer to the preferred level.

Suppose that book retailing is a rapidly consolidating industry, and that your company is growing by making frequent acquisitions of single outlets or small regional chains. While the finance director might be happy to find the cash for one acquisition by taking out a bank loan, when the next acquisition comes along, he or she might decide that it is time to issue shares. It would be wrong to conclude that the first acquisition has been entirely funded by debt (and that the cost of capital for the acquisition is the cost of debt). It would be equally wrong to conclude that the second acquisition has been funded 100 per cent by equity, with a very different cost.

Both acquisitions should be regarded as using the company's 'target' debt/equity ratio and the cost of capital worked out accordingly. They both draw from the same pool of capital. The timing of the funding exercises, which are needed from time to time to keep the mixture at the right strength, must not disguise this underlying reality.

CONCLUSIONS

This chapter has revised the basic principles of project appraisal. It has considered the merits of NPV appraisal based on a project's cash flows. It has discussed the logical basis for using a discount rate (or 'cost of capital') which takes into account both tax effects and the extra returns needed to persuade investors to carry risk.

Defining relevant cash flows

INTRODUCTION

This chapter first discusses the principles involved in measuring project cash flows and then demonstrates them in the context of a case study.

INCREMENTALITY

The project is defined by the *difference* in cash flows between two scenarios – 'accept' and 'reject'. It follows that the future cash flows under both these alternatives must be examined in equal detail. There are psychological forces working against this – there is often enthusiasm for the new project and a lower level of interest in alternatives. Careful and imaginative investigation and analysis of alternatives are vital.

There may be several alternatives. There may be several variants of the project itself. One of the alternatives needs to be identified as the 'base case'. The cash flows of all the alternatives and project variants considered should be measured relative to this. The one that gives the highest Net Present Value (NPV) is the one that should be accepted. This technique works because NPV's are additive. If:

	NPV (Project A relative to 'base-case' C)	= N
and	NPV (Project B relative to 'base-case' C)	= M
then	NPV (Project A relative to Project B)	= N − M

So the alternative with the highest NPV would beat any alternative if they were matched together in a play-off.

Detailed analysis of the cash flows for alternatives is important. Some companies *require* that at least two alternatives are put forward alongside any proposal for capital expenditure and, in most circumstances, this is a good idea. The alternatives may have to include scenarios that are painful to contemplate. At a major textile company, the managers of the mills would send proposals for major reinvestment to head office. The incremental cash flows – relative to carrying on with existing machinery – looked good. Head office had another alternative in mind – close the mill and redevelop the land for other uses. All available choices have to be considered.

The cash flow should attempt to capture all the benefits and disbenefits from a decision. This is not easy to do. Will a project give an introduction to a new market, which might turn out to be very valuable in the long run? Will an acquisition bring new valuable management talent into the company? Will a new contract create a relationship with a major new customer that has the potential to be developed over the long run? Is there a chance that the company might be sued when it puts a new product on the market? It will often be a major exercise of managerial imagination to draw up the list of items that may need to be included.

CASH FLOWS

Problems of cash flow measurement include:

- the treatment of tax payments
- the measurement boundary for cash flows
- the treatment of items that are hard to estimate
- identifying fixed or 'sunk' costs
- inflation
- estimating project life.

Tax payments

For quoted companies, our objective is to accept projects that will push up the market price of the shares. So the cash flows that we want to measure are those that support the share price. These are cash flows after corporate tax, because money that the company has sent to the Inland Revenue has gone just like the money that has been sent to suppliers or workers. If the company could find a way to reduce the corporate tax associated with a project, it would have made that project more valuable.

Personal tax payments are in a different category. The company is not responsible for managing the tax affairs of its investors or debtholders. It does not, in general, know what their status is. If we imagine investors meeting directly to trade shares, personal tax would not enter into the price negotiations. Personal tax payments are not a characteristic of the share; they are characteristic of individual investors and will follow those investors as they make changes in their portfolios. Cash flows are measured after company tax but before personal tax.

It is important to note that the situation might be different for a private company owned by a single individual, the founder. It would be quite logical for this person to look at projects on the basis of 'what will be left for me after all tax charges – corporate and personal – have been paid?' The required rate of return at which these cash flows would be valued would probably differ from the public company case.

Cash flows to whom?

The company gathers capital in the form of debt and equity and uses a mixture of the two to launch the project. When the project is generating cash, this is subject to tax, before being divided between the two types of capital. Figure 3.1 shows a 'full charge' of tax being deducted (i.e. the tax that would be paid using all-equity finance), and then the tax subsidy (i.e. the tax saving from using debt) being re-injected into the cash flow. This breakdown of the tax actually paid is useful in NPV calculations.

Fig. 3.1 The cash flow through a company

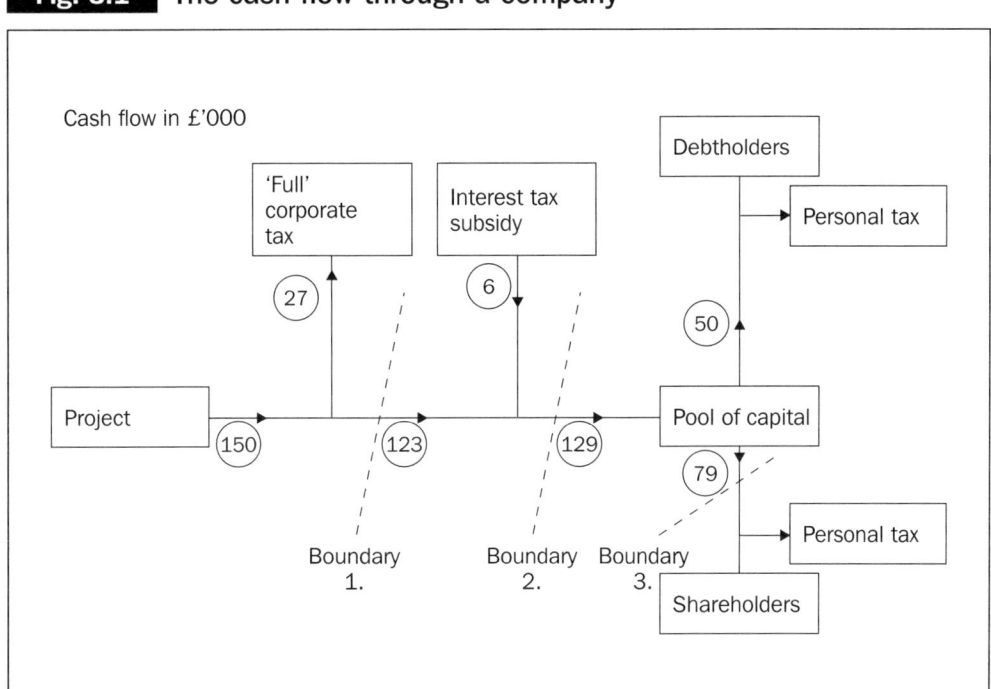

There are three boundaries at which cash flows can be measured, as indicated on Figure 3.1.

- **Boundary 1.** Company cash flow before tax subsidy.
- **Boundary 2.** Company cash flow after tax subsidy.
- **Boundary 3.** Shareholder cash flow before personal tax.

All of these definitions meet our requirement; they are 'after corporate tax and before personal tax'. They can all be used successfully for NPV calculations, although the appropriate discount rate would be different in each case. Shareholder cash flows are riskiest and will require the highest returns.

They must, however, be used consistently. If *company* cash flow is being measured, then the initial outflow is the total amount spent on the project – both shareholders' money and borrowed money. Interest is not subtracted from cash flow, it is part of the cash flow back to the company.

If *equity* cash flow is being measured, then the cash outflow is only the contribution to the project made by shareholders. The subsequent inflow is the amount that comes back to shareholders, i.e. after interest and debt repayments have been subtracted.

The most common choice is a 'company' boundary rather than an 'equity' one. This seems to fit most naturally with the management perspective.

For example, a project involves an initial outlay of £600,000 of which £200,000 is borrowed. In a subsequent year, the cash flow elements (all incremental values) are as follows.

Table 3.1

	£
Sales revenue	500,000
Labour cost	150,000
Materials cost	200,000
Writing down allowance (WDA)	60,000
Interest paid	20,000
Debt repayment	30,000
Taxable income	70,000
Tax at 30%	21,000
After-tax income	49,000

What are the cash flows here? The operating cash flow is £150,000 (sales less labour and materials). Full tax is £27,000 (30 per cent of operating cash flow less WDA). Since actual tax is £21,000, the tax subsidy is identified as £6,000. Of the £129,000 which comes back to the company, £50,000 goes to the debtholders in interest and debt repayment and £79,000 remains for the shareholders. The cash flow numbers are circled on Figure 3.1.

The cash flows at the different boundaries (recognising that we are only considering the inflow for one particular year) are therefore

Boundary		Out	In
1	Company cash-flow before tax subsidy	600,000	123,000
2	Company cash flow after tax subsidy	600,000	129,000
3	Equity cash flow	400,000	79,000

Each of these is a valid measure of cash flow which (with the appropriate discount rate) can be used to calculate NPV. We shall return to consider the choice between them in Chapter 4.

Proxy cash flows

There is a difficulty with our rules for cash-flow measurement. The incrementality rule requires that we capture all the benefits or disbenefits of the project relative to the base case. The cash flow rule requires us to identify the specific inflows and outflows of cash that will occur in each case.

Examination questions on project appraisal are usually carefully worded and information is supplied to convert every positive or negative feature of the investment into a set of cash flows. Real-life projects do not have the same convenient properties.

Wherever there is a clash between including all benefits/disbenefits and counting only readily identifiable cash flows, opt to include the benefits. If necessary, fudge the cash flows by putting in an estimate of an appropriate number. You may need to draw attention to the crude assumption that you have made, but it is better, if at all possible, to include some number to represent a consequence of the project (a number that may trigger healthy debate), than to ignore the factor or relegate it to verbal recognition in a footnote.

Example

A fast-growing company is considering changing its production techniques so that it will need to hold fewer components in stock. This will liberate space in the warehouse. The company expects that it will need to acquire additional warehouse space in a year or two, but no detailed planning for this has been undertaken and in any case, the timing is uncertain and will depend on how its business develops. The project will postpone the need for additional warehouse space.

Should these facts relating to the warehouse be included as an element of project cash flow? If so, how?

The saving of warehouse space is a genuine benefit, which should not be ignored. However, the incremental cash flows from the benefit are hard to identify. It would be necessary to decide how large an extension to the warehouse will be built – and when, and at what cost – if the project goes ahead, and then to do the same thing on the assumption that the project does not go ahead. These numbers might be very large in relation to all the other cash flow elements and getting estimates might be a complex, time-consuming job.

Why not simply impute a value to each square metre of warehouse space liberated? Estimates of the market rental of warehouse space will not be difficult to obtain. This might be inappropriate. If the company had a permanent surplus of warehouse space available (and it is hard to see why management should tolerate this situation) then liberating warehouse space would *not* be a benefit and this item should be ignored. It is also possible that the company is operating in cramped premises and that the gain from liberating warehouse space is significantly greater than the market rental value of space in the general neighbourhood. But, these special cases apart, using a market value proxy may be the most practical approach available and, there are certainly many situations where it can be justified.

Fixed costs and sunk costs

'Ignore fixed costs' is a well-known rule for project appraisal. Fixed costs will not vary whether or not the project is accepted. So they can be left out of the analysis. This rule can easily be misapplied. The main problem is that 'fixed costs' can mean two different things.

- *Fixed costs are costs that do not vary with the volume of production.* There are many such costs. The costs of renting retail premises may well be a fixed sum, independent of the level of sales achieved. The breakdown of costs into fixed and variable is a basic element of a management accountant's job.

- *Fixed costs are costs that cannot be varied over time.* Project appraisal is concerned with cash flows over time. If we are going to treat costs as 'fixed' in project appraisal terms, we are assuming that they cannot be varied over a time span that, for most projects, covers several years. How many costs have this characteristic?

My colleague teaches an MBA programme with me. Any student who mentions the term 'fixed costs' to him is in for a rough ride. 'Fixed costs!' says my colleague 'What fixed costs? You show me fixed costs and I'll show you incompetent management.'

Of course, he is referring to the second type of fixed costs. His point is that good management is unlikely to burden a company with costs which, in the long or medium term, cannot be varied. Good management will find a way to adjust the size of the workforce, or the amount of floor space used, to the current needs of the business.

Any claim that a cost is fixed over a substantial time period should be viewed with suspicion. The cry of 'fixed costs' can be a very misleading one. The same is true for sunk costs. Sunk costs are payments which the company has made, or is already irrevocably committed to making, and which cannot be recouped.

Example

A company is planning to extend its factory as part of a project to expand its product line. It would use land that it bought many years ago at the time the factory was originally built. So, when appraising the project, is the land a 'sunk cost', which should be ignored?

No. It is true that the price originally paid is irrelevant, but the land will have a current market value. If it is not used for the current project it could be sold. So the incremental cost becomes the market price. Perhaps the sale of the land is not the appropriate alternative. The company would plan to keep the land, but if it is retained, this can only be because the land is judged to be worth at least its current market price to the company. It might be that land for expansion adjacent to the current operation is judged to be essential for highly profitable projects, which seem likely to crop up in the future – and it should not be wasted on a marginally profitable project today, even if the project can afford to 'pay' the open market value. So current market price is a minimum cost for the land in the NPV calculation.

A good example of a 'sunk' cost would be the cost of the architect's plans for the extension to the factory. These may be needed at an early stage so that proper costing and analysis of the project can be carried out. Once they are commissioned, the cost is 'sunk' and plays no further part in the calculations. Someone, of course, must make the original judgement that the project is sufficiently interesting to justify the cost of detailed architectural work.

Inflation

In the last quarter of the 20th century, annual inflation in the UK has been above 20 per cent and below 1 per cent. Its prospects in the 21st century are uncertain.

Inflation can make a major difference to cash flows. At 7 per cent inflation, a constant-purchasing-power cash flow will double over a decade in money terms. For long-lived projects, the inflation assumption can be a crucial part of the appraisal.

It is tempting to ignore inflation and to assume that current prices will continue. Since inflation often helps projects, growing the revenue line faster than costs, ignoring inflation can seem a cautious, conservative policy but it can easily delude companies into passing up good investment opportunities.

All the elements that contribute to project cash flow should incorporate the likely future course of inflation, and should take into account other factors that will change their value over time. Wage and salary levels have a tendency to rise 2–2.5 per cent above the rate of inflation. The prices of manufactured goods – electronic consumer goods in particular – have tended to rise by less than inflation.

The best way to estimate future inflation is by observing the available returns on risk-free Government bonds. The UK Government issues both conventional bonds (where future payments are fixed in money terms) and index-linked bonds (where future payments will be up-rated in line with inflation). The interest rates on the conventional and index linked bonds (N and R respectively) appear in the financial press every day. The difference between N (the 'nominal' rate) and R (the 'real' rate) is the market forecast of inflation (I). The short-cut formula is:

$$I = N - R$$

Technically, the accurate version of the relationship is:

$$1 + I = \frac{1 + N}{1 + R}$$

$$\text{and } I = \frac{1 + N}{1 + R} - 1$$

Suppose we are interested in forecasting inflation over a five-year period starting in early 2000. The redemption yield on conventional stock (N) maturing in 2006 is 6.26 per cent. The yield on index-linked stock (R) maturing in 2006 is 2.34 per cent. On this basis, the 'short-cut' formula gives an inflation forecast of 3.92 per cent. The accurate version gives 3.83 per cent. The error from using the short-cut formula would be more significant if the forecast rate of inflation was higher.

This method of forecasting is as good as any but, historically, all methods of forecasting inflation have performed poorly. Inflation might turn out to be much higher, or much lower, and this appears to generate a large risk element in the NPV calculations. In fact, if inflation is higher than forecast, interest rates are likely to be higher, too. A large component of interest rates is compensation to savers for inflation. So although the cash flows in future years will be higher than expected, the appropriate discount rate for converting them to present value will be higher too. The effects may tend to offset each other.

Some appraisals are carried out on the following basis:

■ Predict future cash flows on the basis of the current price level. Ignore forecasts of future inflation.

■ Remove the inflation element from the discount rate by using R, not N as the basic risk-free rate.

This can be described as a 'consistent' approach, because the inflation element has been taken out of the numerator and the denominator of the NPV calculation. But it still has problems. Tax authorities do not work on an inflation-adjusted basis, so the forecasts of future tax payments will be very poor. Inflation tends to increase the tax burden on companies and projects. Governments can find it convenient for this reason. The best cash flow forecasts must incorporate the best available inflation forecasts.

When will the project end?

It is often difficult to predict how long a project will last or the circumstances in which it will be terminated. Sometimes the project will involve buying equipment which is known to last for N years, or it may involve taking a lease on a building for M years. These numbers then set the project life for appraisal purposes.

This is a mistake. As explained in Chapter 1, project life is rarely linked to the life of equipment. A project is an economic opportunity which will last until demand changes or technology changes or relative prices change, etc. These events are difficult to predict. A project should not be identified with a particular asset or assets. A piece of machinery will operate until it rusts, or its bearings give out, or it loses its tolerances but we cannot assume that these events will terminate the project.

Tobacco companies in the UK are very long established businesses. Their brands, distribution capability, and ability to maintain product quality have all been sources of competitive advantage which has enabled their basic cigarette manufacturing activity to continue profitably for several generations. The actual machinery used to manufacture the cigarettes will have been replaced many times over that period. Asset life has very little relationship to project life.

There are three main solutions to the project-life problem.

■ Estimate a terminal date for cash flows from the project.

■ Assume that the project is 'sold' and generates a proxy cash flow at the end of a fixed period – say 10 years. The project is 'sold' for a multiple of the profits that it is generating at that time. This technique is particularly useful where the project is a corporate acquisition. The acquired business is expected to continue to operate on a long-term basis, but some practical bound to the cash flow sequence has to be set.

■ Assume that a project will continue indefinitely and express its benefit as a constant annual cash flow. These 'annualised cost' techniques are explained in detail in Chapter 7.

AN ILLUSTRATION OF THE PROBLEMS OF CASH FLOW DEFINITION

Case study 3.1

Thomsen Seating plc

Thomsen Seating is a supplier of seats to the automobile industry. It has supplied seats for Nisada cars for a number of years, and is considering whether to take up an offer to be the supplier for the new Quasar model which will go into production in 2002. It is being offered the right of first refusal on the contract, but under new conditions.

■ Nisada is demanding a 9 per cent price cut, from £210 to £191, in the price of a set of seats. Nisada plans to make 170,000 of the new model each year. The new model will have a life of six years before it, in turn, will be replaced.

- Nisada is suggesting that Thomsen should move its seat production onto the site of where the cars are manufactured. Nisada is putting this forward as a way of 'helping' Thomsen to meet the new price target. Thomsen would rent 5,000 sq.ft. of space under a six-year contract at £10 per sq.ft. per year with yearly rental payments at the beginning of each year and a rent review after three years. Thomsen would also purchase two automatic frame-welding machines, to a specification set by Nisada. In certain events of default, Nisada could remove Thomsen from the contract, acquire the machinery at a written-down value, and bring in another seat manufacturer to complete the contract. Each machine would cost £30,000 and would be fully written off for tax purposes over six years. They would each have an estimated market value of £3,000 at the end of six years and Nisada has the right to acquire them at this price.

- From Thomsen's point of view, a switch to in-plant manufacturing would liberate 5,000 sq.ft. of space in its own plant. It would be possible to sell this space as a separate factory unit for £600,000. Alternatively, it could be rented out to yield Thomsen £50,000 per year next year. However, Thomsen's management has a preference for keeping the space, as it would give an opportunity for expansion.

- In-plant manufacture would reduce the inventory of finished seats from two days' supply to less than one day. The value of inventory would fall by £230,000. Thomsen would need to sell two of its current frame-welding machines. The machines, which cost £20,000 each two years ago, currently have a written down value of £12,000 each. However, the market for such equipment is limited, and it was estimated that they could only be sold for £8,000 (each). The machines could stay in service for a further six years, and if so, they would be worth £2,000 each on disposal.

- Production of seats for the new Quasar would require 60 production employees including supervisors. Fifty current employees had expressed a willingness to move their place of work. Ten current staff would be offered redundancy and ten new staff recruited to take their place. The cost of enhanced pension and severance rights for the redundant workers is calculated by the actuaries to be £120,000. However, the actuaries have also calculated that Thomsen's pension scheme is currently in surplus and that the payments can be funded without any increase in contributions to the scheme by employer or employees.

- Thomsen's financial policy is to finance 50 per cent of its working capital through bank loans and 25 per cent of its fixed assets. The interest rate is 12 per cent. The corporate tax rate is 40 per cent.

The problem

Thomsen wants to decide whether to supply Nisada from its current factory or to move to in-plant manufacture. What are the incremental cash flows associated with this decision?

In this example we shall use the 'Boundary 2' cash flow definition.

Solution

We shall consider separately each of the main elements of the proposed deal. Retaining the current manufacturing system is the 'base case'. In-plant manufacture is the project.

The price reduction

This is an easy one. Thomsen has to make the price reduction whether it manufactures in its own factory or moves to Nisada's plant. There is no cash flow which is incremental to the decision. So the price reduction can be ignored in the analysis.

If Thomsen were to change the question, and ask whether it was worthwhile accepting Nisada's business at all, then the new price would certainly be relevant. But it is not relevant for the project as defined.

Space

The charge for using Nisada's in-house facilities is straightforward at £50,000 per year. Notice that the rent is to be reviewed (i.e. reset to market level) after three years. It is impossible to forecast the new level accurately, but a reasonable approach would be to assume that the rent will rise in line with inflation. If the inflation forecast, calculated by the method described earlier, is 5 per cent, then the annual rent for the second three-year period would be estimated at

$$50,000 \ (1.05)^3 = 57,880$$

This amount would, of course, be tax deductible.

The gain from liberating space in Thomsen's existing factory is harder to measure. There are two possibilities.

First, assume that the space is sold on a freehold basis to a third party. This would bring in £600,000 (of which a capital gain element would be subject to tax). Note, however, that to be in the same position as the 'base-case' at the end of six years, it would be necessary to re-acquire the property in year six. If we assume that property prices rise in line with inflation, the pre-tax cash flows would be:

Year 0	Year 1	Year 2	Year 3	Year 4	Year 5	Year 6
+600,000						−804,060

Alternatively, the proxy-cash flows could be the notional rental. This amount could be expected to rise at 5 per cent per year, giving taxable cash flows of

Year 0	Year 1	Year 2	Year 3	Year 4	Year 5	Year 6
	50,000	52,500	55,125	57,881	60,775	63,814

Of these two proxies for the value of liberated space, the second is certainly more attractive. The cash flows involved in selling and repurchasing the property (including the associated tax) are a difficult and indirect approach to the problem.

Note, however, that values higher than the estimated rental might well be justified. The fact that Thomsen does not plan to sell or find a tenant for the property implies that the space is worth *at least* the estimated forgone rental. If Thomsen had been turning away attractive business because of lack of space, then the value to Thomsen might be considerably above the open market rental. The higher value would be the appropriate one to use in the appraisal calculation.

It would be quite wrong to treat Thomsen's factory as a fixed cost and to place no value on the liberated space.

Working capital

When a project requires an increase in working capital, then it absorbs cash. When a project makes it possible to reduce working capital, as in this case, it liberates cash. This project generates an inflow of £230,000 in year zero.

In year six, however, the project gives Thomsen £230,000 less working capital to liquidate or to roll forward into future projects. The project can only be placed in the same position as the 'base case' by an outflow of £230,000 in year six. The general pattern of a working-capital line is an initial entry balanced by a terminal entry of opposite sign.

Inflation affects working capital. A small adjustment is needed each year. In this case a small saving is made each year, because the stock of working capital which has to be inflation-adjusted each year is smaller if the project is accepted. The working capital line becomes

Year 0	Year 1	Year 2	Year 3	Year 4	Year 5	Year 6
230,000	11,500	12,075	12,679	13,313	13,978	(293,545)

Note that cash outflows to increase working capital are not tax deductable, and cash inflows from reducing working capital are tax free.

Machinery

For the two new frame-welding machines, the pre-tax cash flows are

Year 0	Year 1	Year 2	Year 3	Year 4	Year 5	Year 6
(60,000)						6,000

The tax allowances in each year (recorded as negative quantities, since they are deductions from taxable income) are

Year 0	Year 1	Year 2	Year 3	Year 4	Year 5	Year 6
	(10,000)	(10,000)	(10,000)	(10,000)	(10,000)	(4,000)

In year six, tax allowances of £10,000 could have been claimed if the machines had been scrapped as valueless at the end of the year. Since they are sold for £6,000, only a £4,000 'loss of value' can be claimed.

For Thomsen's current machines which are to be sold the cash proceeds in year 0 will be £16,000 while cash proceeds of £4,000 from disposal in year 6 will be forgone. Since the machines have a book value of £24,000, Thomsen will give up tax allowances that it would have received of

Year 0	Year 1	Year 2	Year 3	Year 4	Year 5	Year 6
	6,000	6,000	6,000	6,000		

and will instead get a single allowance relating to the loss on sale of £8,000 in year one. Putting these items together, and recognising that the forgone disposal proceeds in year six would have been taxable, we have tax adjustments relating to the old machinery as

Year 0	Year 1	Year 2	Year 3	Year 4	Year 5	Year 6
	(2,000)	6,000	6,000	6,000		(4,000)

We are assuming that, in the base case, Thomsen does not buy a new machine in year five. The old machine continues to give satisfactory service although it is fully written down. Note that the rules governing tax allowances are complex, and this briefing does not attempt to cover them. The allowances in this example are on a straight-line basis, although reducing balance is common in the UK. First-year allowances are not normally available in the UK, although they have been available in the past (in the example, the 'old machinery' has benefited from such a system).

Redundancy

The £120,000 cost of redundancies will be met by the Thomsen pension scheme. Can this item, then, be ignored in the appraisal?

No. A company and its pension scheme are intimately linked financially. The company is committed to making up any shortfall in the fund. A surplus in the fund can, under certain circumstances, be returned to the company. The £120,000 should be treated as a tax-deductible expenditure, because contributions to approved pension schemes are, in general, deductible for tax purposes. The after-tax amount will be £120,000$(1 - t)$ = £72,000 and this cost will be entered in the cash flow calculations.

Interest payments

If we are measuring cash flows at company level then interest payments are not themselves a cash outflow. They are a payment made out of the company cash inflow – like dividends. However, it is necessary to calculate the interest payments if we want to calculate the tax subsidy.

Thomsen's policy is to finance 50 per cent of its working capital with debt at 12 per cent. Working capital has fallen by £230,000, so debt will fall by £115,000 and annual interest payments by £13,800. With a tax rate of 40 per cent, the project will mean that Thomsen will lose a tax subsidy of £13,800 $\times$ 0.40 = £5,520 in the first year. This amount will rise with inflation.

Thomsen also has a policy of using debt to finance fixed assets, measured presumably by their balance sheet value. The project requires that Thomsen replace two partly written-down machines with two new ones. The level and pattern over time of fixed assets in the balance sheet will change.

The effect will not be large; it will be far smaller than the working capital charge. It will often be necessary to judge a particular aspect of a project to be immaterial. We shall do so in this case, and shall not attempt to calculate the change in the pattern of tax subsidies associated with the fixed interest debt. Judgements of this sort are essential in real-world appraisals.

The calculation of the incremental tax associated with the project is shown in Table 3.2.

Table 3.2 The tax calculation

Tax calculation	yr 0	yr 1	yr 2	yr 3	yr 4	yr 5	yr 6	yr 7
Rental of in-plant space		−50,000	−50,000	−50,000	−57,881	−57,881	−57,881	
Imputed rent of liberated space		50,000	52,550	55,125	57,881	60,775	63,814	
Tax allowances new machinery		−10,000	−10,000	−10,000	−10,000	−10,000	−4,000	
Tax adjustments old machinery		−2,000	6,000	6,000	6,000		−4,000	
Incremental interest		13,800	14,490	15,215	15,975	16,774	17,617	
Taxable income		1,800	13,040	16,340	11,975	9,668	15,550	
Tax cash flow at 40%			−720	−5,216	−6,536	−4,790	−3,867	−6,220

This presentation shows a lag of one year in the tax payment system. Using annual cash flows, it is easiest to illustrate the tax delay in this way. For large companies in the UK the delay is shorter than this, and a substantial part of the tax bill is currently settled on a quarterly basis. The tax rate of 40 per cent is purely illustrative. The rate is currently substantially lower than this for large companies, and lower still for small ones. It has varied over time in the past and is likely to continue to do so in the future.

Incremental project cash flows

After this lengthy analysis the components of cash flow can now be put together, as shown in Table 3.3.

Table 3.3

Project cash flow	yr 0	yr 1	yr 2	yr 3	yr 4	yr 5	yr 6	yr 7
Rental of in-plant space	−50,000	−50,000	−50,000	−57,881	−57,881	−57,881		
Imputed rent of liberated space		50,000	52,550	55,125	57,881	60,775	63,814	
New machines – acquisition and disposal	−60,000						6,000	
Early disposal of old machines	16,000						−4,000	
Working capital	230,000	11,500	12,075	12,679	13,313	13,978	−293,545	
Redundancy	−72,000							
Tax cash flow at 40%			−720	−5,216	−6,536	−4,790	−3,867	−6,220
Incremental project cash flow	64,000	11,500	13,905	4,707	6,777	12,082	−231,598	−6,220

With a 10 per cent required return, this project does not look attractive. The NPV is −£160,310. Notice, incidentally, that this is a 'reverse cash flow' project with inflows first and outflows later. For such a project, a high IRR is bad news as explained in chapter 2. The IRR is 16.1 per cent, higher than the required rate, but this does not mean that the project adds value. The negative NPV tells the true story.

Beyond cash flow

We have now set out the identifiable incremental cash flows from the project. Is the job done? No. The next task is to consider whether the cash flows that we have identified have captured all the significant benefits and disbenefits that the company will get from the project. In the context of the Thomsen case, it looks as though there are some major ones we have omitted.

Why did Nisada say that they wanted Thomsen to move in-plant? It was to achieve better quality control. Better quality control has not figured in the cash flows at all. If Thomsen rejects this argument completely, the treatment is correct. But if there is some validity to the point, shouldn't it appear in the analysis in some way?

Consider the potential scale of any quality effect. If Nisada were correct and the scrappage rate could be halved from 0.4 per cent to 0.2 per cent, then the annual saving, estimated at the new prices would be

$$0.002 \times 170,000 \times £191 = £64,940$$

What is it worth to Thomsen to find out whether savings on this scale are obtainable? If in-plant manufacture does turn out to bring important quality benefits, and competitors adapt more quickly, how damaging could that be for Thomsen's business? Could Thomson, with no in-plant experience, find itself at a disadvantage pitching for business against competitors who can demonstrate success at this manufacturing method?

These risks are vague and very difficult to quantify. But some sort of quantification must be attempted if these factors are to be rationally considered.

Do we judge that there is an *X*% chance that in-plant manufacturing will turn out to be a success, and that, if so, a proportion of Thomsen's business yielding *Y* in annual net cash flow would be at risk over a period of *Z* years (i.e. until Thomsen had acquired and could demonstrate competence at the new technique)?

If X was 20 per cent, Y was £1.5m and Z was three years, then the 'expected loss' from failing to experiment with in-plant manufacture (assuming a 12 per cent discount rate) would be

$$\frac{1.5m*0.2}{1.12} + \frac{1.5m*0.2}{(1.12)^2} + \frac{1.5m*0.2}{(1.12)^3} = 720,549$$

This is large enough to make a difference to the decision. It is very uncertain, but it might be the best available estimate. The management analysis of this project should centre on values of X, Y and Z which are clearly in this example far more important than investigating the likely disposal value of machinery at the end of the project's life.

Quality is not the only 'background issue' in this case. There is manufacturing flexibility. If Nisada stops its assembly line for any reason, work on seat manufacture will have to stop as soon as the limited storage space is filled. When Thomsen manufactures in its own factory, workers often can be switched from one order to another. How much paid-but-unworked time does Thomsen have in relation to its current work for Nisada? How much might it be for an in-house plant? The difference is an estimated loss that should be charged to the project.

CONCLUSIONS

This chapter has discussed the principles involved in setting out project cash flows. These principles have then been illustrated, at some length, in the Thomsen case study. The Thomsen example has also been used to demonstrate other important truths about cash flow analysis.

Economists are fond of the 'lost keys' story. A man walking home one night meets a neighbour who is poking around with his hand close to the ground under a street light. 'What's the matter?' 'I've lost my keys' replies the neighbour. So the man pitches in and starts hunting around to see if he can spot any keys but without success.

'Are you sure you dropped them here?' he asks. 'Oh no' replies the neighbour. 'I dropped them somewhere over there. But the light is better here.'

In the same way, there is a tendency to use numbers in financial analysis that are easy to get and to ignore highly relevant numbers which may be very difficult to estimate. The Thomsen case has illustrated this. The readily forecastable numbers, calculated in detail, gave a modestly negative NPV for the project. Consideration of broader (but highly uncertain) consequences of the project generated positive estimates that were considerably larger in magnitude, and which, in this case, would be decisive. Cash flow analysis is not a neat and tidy job. It is often, inevitably, vague and messy. Some of the numbers may be highly debatable – indeed they should be vigorously debated within the company. It is much more important to be broadly correct – putting rough numbers to all of the significant consequences of the project – than to be precisely wrong by confining the analysis to numbers that can be accurately foreseen and estimated.

4

Risk-adjusted returns

INTRODUCTION

This chapter discusses how the underlying theory relating required return to risk can be applied in practice and considers:

- required returns for projects that are 'typical' of the company's activities
- required returns for unquoted companies
- divisional required returns
- project-specific required returns, for projects which are not typical of the company's activities.

All this discussion will be based on the logic of the Capital Asset Pricing Model, which was introduced in Chapter 2. The central point is that the required return for any set of cash flows is directly related to the β associated with these flows. The β is the sensitivity of the market value of the flows to movements in the stock market index. β values for the shares of quoted companies are readily available from published sources.

REQUIRED RETURNS FOR TYPICAL PROJECTS

Let us take Marks and Spencer plc as an example. The β of Marks and Spencer shares can be directly obtained from various sources. In 1999, the London Business School's Risk Measurement Service gave the β as 0.94. The risk-free interest (on Treasury Bills) was 5.8 per cent. We use the historic equity risk premium of 6.5 per cent. So the CAPM tells us that investors are expecting a return of 11.9 per cent when they buy Marks and Spencer shares and Marks and Spencer management should not use shareholders' money for new projects unless they believe that they can match this expectation. Using the CAPM formula

$$\text{Expected Return} = \text{Risk free rate} + [\beta \times \text{Equity Risk Premium}]$$
$$5.8\% + (0.94 \times 6.5\%)$$
$$= 11.9\%$$

This is a required return on equity capital. If Marks and Spencer management measures cash flows at equity level, then this is the appropriate discount rate to use in NPV calculations.

It is more likely that cash flows will be measured on a company basis. Cash outflows are measured from the pool of capital (from both shareholders and debtholders) and the cash inflows are the amounts that come back to the pool.

Company cash flows are less risky than equity cash flows. Company cash flows are divided into a risk-rich flow for the shareholders and a (nearly) risk-free flow to the debtholders. The risk-level of company cash flows is a blend of these two components. Hence the β of company cash flows is a blend of Equity β and Debt β. At Boundary 2, the weighted average formula gives

$$\beta_2 = \begin{bmatrix} \text{Equity proportion } * \ \beta \\ \text{of total value} \qquad \text{Equity} \end{bmatrix} + \begin{bmatrix} \text{Debt proportion } * \ \beta \\ \text{of total capital} \qquad \text{Debt} \end{bmatrix}$$

Total capital is equity plus debt (E + D). Hence

$$\beta_2 = \frac{E}{E + D} * \beta_E$$

To calculate the β of the cash flows at Boundary 1, we argue as follows. The tax subsidy is a low risk cash flow like the interest payments. It will be received as long as the company is making a taxable profit. The tax subsidy can be regarded as contributing (T*D) to the value of the company's debt. If the tax subsidy was subtracted from the interest payments, the value of the debt would fall to (1-T)*D. If follows that the cash inflows at Boundary 1 could be split into (1-T)*D of debt and E of equity. So the weighted average β at this boundary is

$$\beta_1 = \frac{E}{E + D(1 - T)} * \beta_E$$

β1 has a name. It is called the 'Asset β' of the company. It is a measure which depends only on the operating risk of the company's business and not at all on the company's debt policy. Equity β depends on both the risk of the company's business and the degree to which this risk has been geared up by using debt.

Returning to our example, if for Marks and Spencer £3,140m is the appropriately measured value of equity (E), and £1,005m the value of the debt (D), then the β values for company cash flows at the different boundaries are shown in Fig. 4.1. The assumed tax rate is 31 per cent. The required returns follow directly from the βs using the CAPM formula.

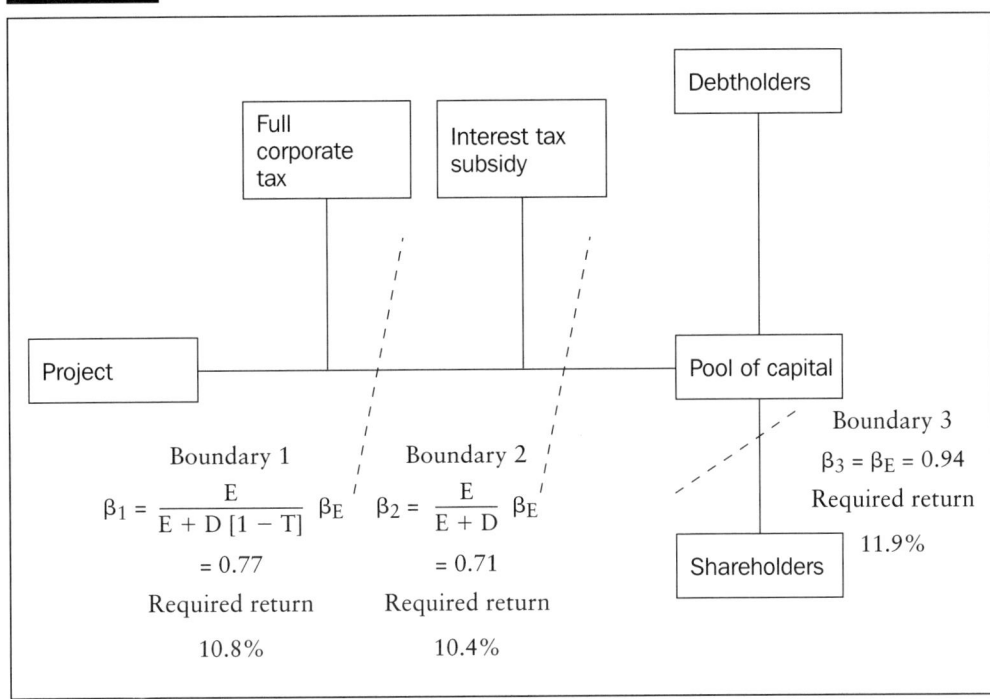

Fig. 4.1 ß values for company cash flows

The accuracy of ß measurement

For a quoted company the basic source will be a β book such as that produced by the London Business School (LBS). A β co-efficient is measured by a process of statistical inference. Even if the gearing and the operating characteristics of the business have stayed content, β is measured with statistical error. The LBS service gives the error. For Marks and Spencer the β is 0.94 and the standard error 0.13. This means that, although 0.94 is the best available estimate, there is a 1 in 6 chance that the true β is more than 0.94 + 0.13 = 1.07 and a 1 in 6 chance that it is less than 0.94 − 0.13 = 0.81. Even this calculation overstates the accuracy with which we know β, because changes in the financial and operating structure of the business have not been taken into account.

Since the average β is 1, βs that are a long way from unity are slightly suspect. Another way to check whether your β has been strongly influenced by statistical error is to imagine that your company is unquoted and to calculate the β indirectly as explained below.

Seeing the size of errors in β calculations should have a salutary effect. We shall set required rates of return as accurately as we can; but, clearly, this is not going to be a highly precise process.

Unquoted companies

If your own company is unquoted, the best source of information will be the β of other quoted companies in the same industry. The LBS gives average βs for a variety of industries. However, these are only useful if levels of gearing are uniform throughout the industry.

A further difficulty is that the term 'industry' can cover a very wide variety of activities. 'Insurance' can cover both property insurance companies and life insurers. The risk characteristics of these activities are very different. 'Engineering' can include companies with advanced, unique technology and others which may produce standard automobile components. 'Retailers' can include companies which own their own stores (which are a major components of company value) and companies whose policy is to rent. Again, the risk characteristics will be very different.

The most appropriate technique is to choose a few 'comparators' – quoted companies with business activities closely similar to your own – and average them. It is the Asset βs, not the Equity βs that will be closely similar. So the procedure involves acquiring the Equity βs and gearing ratios of the comparator firms; calculating the Asset βs; averaging these numbers; and taking this as an estimate of your own Asset β. If necessary, this can be used to calculate your Equity β.

DIFFICULTIES IN CALCULATING RISK-ADJUSTED REQUIRED RETURNS

Problem 1: Measuring debt and equity

The values of debt (D) and equity (E) are required for the calculation of company βs. There are two ways in which they can be measured – at market value or at book value. Both measurements can lead to errors, especially in the measurement of E, and it is a matter of judgement which approach, in a particular case, is likely to lead to a smaller error.

The use of book (accounting) values leads to errors because accountants value assets in eccentric ways, such as applying arbitrary depreciation schedules, failing to incorporate inflation, ignoring assets such as patents or brands, etc.

Market values also have problems. A large part of equity value is justified by the opportunities that the company may have to make profitable opportunities in the future. Some illustrative calculations in chapter 1 showed that this factor can account for a large part of value for 'normal' companies; and for 'growth' or 'technology' companies it can account for the great majority of the equity value.

Suppose that such a company followed a rigid policy of funding all its investment projects equally with debt and equity, so that the appropriate gearing ratio for assessing the tax subsidy associated with a new project was D/E = 1. This ratio would be roughly reflected in the book values of D and E, but market values could give a very different ratio because of the 'future opportunities' element in E.

If we accept that the difference between the market value of equity and the book value is largely due to 'long-term future opportunities', and that the actual operations of the company are financed by debt and equity in roughly book value proportions, then the use of book value to measure D and E can be justified as the lesser of two evils.

This briefing, therefore, tends to the use of book value weights in the required return formulas. There are exceptions; 'future opportunities' cannot have a negative value, so if book value of equity exceeds market value this must indicate that the accounting system is overstating the real economic value of the assets. In this case, market value weights would be preferred. In general, if you believe that the accounting system has done a notably poor job of measuring the economic value of the company's assets, or if you believe future growth opportunities are insignificant, the case for using market values becomes stronger.

Problem 2: Is debt risk-free?

Companies rarely default on their debt, but that is not the same as being risk-free from our perspective. We have taken the β of debt to be zero. This is reasonably accurate for short-term debt, but the value of long-term fixed interest debt can be relative – its value moves inversely with the level of interest rates. Generally, the equity market shares this characteristic, so long-term bonds have a positive β and, the longer the term the higher the β. Debt βs are available and they can be incorporated in the averaging process that calculates the β of corporate cash flows. However, unless long-term debt makes up a substantial proportion of the capital structure, this refinement is usually ignored.

Problem 3: What is the equity risk premium?

We have already referred to the historic UK equity premium of 6.5 per cent, measured over an 80-year period. The longer the period, the smaller the statistical error in the measurement and 1918 is as far back as good records are available.

Criticisms of historic value

However, there is still considerable doubt about the current value of the ERP. And since the ERP is a large component of most required return calculations, we need to consider the criticisms of the historic value that have been proposed.

Criticism 1: An ERP of 6.5 per cent is not credible in the long run. Share returns are made up of two parts; dividends and capital gains. If share prices rise over the long run in line with the growth of the economy (say 2.5 per cent real) then capital gains will also be 2.5 per cent. In early 2000, the dividend yield on the stock market index is roughly 2.5 per cent, so the total real return on this basis is

$$2.5\% + 2.5\% = 5.0\%$$

Since the risk-free real rate is 2.0 per cent, the equity risk premium must be roughly 3.0 per cent. This is a neat argument which crops up frequently. It is true that the value of the stock market must, over the very long run, grow at a similar rate to the economy. But long-term capital gains need not be limited in this way. Cash takeovers, share buybacks and other events can mean that the aggregate capital gains in the market are not measured by the change in the total value of shares from one year's end to the next. Takeover and buybacks have taken place and continue to take place on a large scale. The argument is fundamentally flawed.

Criticism 2: The character of the market has changed enormously over 80 years. What relevance does data from so far back have? Eighty years ago, investment in ordinary shares was only for the brave. Regulation of the market was weak and malpractice (by present standards) widespread. Surely a substantially lower risk premium is demanded in today's cleaned-up markets?

There are two issues here. Measured risk has not declined substantially over the decades, although there is evidence that fair weather periods are interspersed with stock market storms in which volatility can rise dramatically. However, a one-off rise in share prices due to the creation of fairer, better-regulated markets is certainly possible. If this factor had doubled prices (which seems a very generous assessment) it would account for less than 1 per cent per year of stock market return. So we cannot argue that the historic ERP is likely to be substantially overstated for this reason.

Criticism 3: Who won the wars? The victors write the history books. The ERP may be large in the US and the UK, but what about Germany and Japan? It is certainly true that German equity investors suffered a very poor experience in the earlier half of the 20th century, but surely a repetition of their experience is now very unlikely for any investor anywhere?

Another significant 'victory' for investors has been the decline of communism and other anti-capitalist forces. Left-of-centre governments are now very happy to praise entrepreneurship and to talk of the importance of 'private sector discipline'. This political shift is another one-off development which has helped investor returns in the past and which will not recur – and which may make historic equity returns an upwardly biased estimate of future returns. However, the historic ERP in the US, where anti-capitalist political forces have never been strong, is closely similar to that in the UK. This suggests the bias is unlikely to be substantial.

Criticism 4: The effect of inflation. One of the reasons the historic ERP is so high is that risk-free returns have been so low. Over the 80-year period, they have averaged only 1.6 per cent in real terms. In particular, real risk-free returns were very low for a period in the 1970s and 1980s when inflation was high. Again, this is cited as a one-off event which has pushed the historic ERP to an unsustainable level.

Risk-free real returns can be observed on a forward-looking basis for the UK. Data from the gilts suggest a long-term rate of about 2 per cent. So, possibly, the historic measurement of ERP might be an overstatement by about 0.4 per cent. This would assume that the forces depressing risk-free returns were not simultaneously depressing equity returns.

Criticism 5: A zero risk-premium. Over long time-periods, ordinary shares have always outperformed risk-free investments. So why should there be a risk premium at all? Because, of course, although stock markets continue indefinitely, people do not. People have a relatively short savings horizon and do indeed find shares to be riskier assets than bank deposits.

This brief survey shows that many ingenious arguments have been devised which claim the historic ERP is an overestimate. This might, of course, be caused by bias among those active in the debate. A low ERP justifies high share prices and large takeover-bid premiums.

To conclude this section, there seems little justification to use an ERP that is far away from the historic average. The various arguments, coupled with the knowledge that the ERP is measured with a statistical error, might persuade some finance directors to use a value of, perhaps, 1 per cent below the historic average. However, the historic average is certainly the best hard measure that we have – and the safest approach is to stick closely to it

Problem 4: Is ß dead?

Reports that the Capital Asset Pricing Model has been discredited appear from time to time. It is true that empirical tests designed to demonstrate the expected relationship between β and return have often failed to do so. This might indicate that there is something wrong with the underlying model, or it might indicate that the methodology of the tests and the power of the tests are insufficient.

The theory of the CAPM is very soundly based on the logic of human risk-aversion. It is difficult to test, partly because, in a very risky environment, claims about investors' expectations have to be tested against actual out-turns. At present, the general consensus is that CAPM is a highly useful model – indeed, it is the best practical model available for setting required returns. Work is continuing both on theory and empirical testing and it is certainly possible that the current model may be revised and improved in the future.

PROJECT-SPECIFIC RETURNS

One insight that has been gained from the CAPM is that the required return on any capital investment should be related to the risk of the investment. There is really no such thing as a required return for a company. Unless all the company's projects happen to have the same risk, the company should use a range of required returns tailored to the nature of each individual investment.

There are several ways of doing this:

- divisional required returns

- project classifications

- project analysis method.

Divisional required returns

Many large companies are made up of divisions, and the divisions themselves may operate in different industrial sectors. A company may, for example, be involved in pharmaceutical manufacture as well as running a chain of chemists' shops. It may operate breweries and also own hotels. The risk characteristics of these operations may differ substantially. In this case, an appropriate solution is to treat each division as a separate unquoted company and use the procedure described under *Unquoted companies* on page 54. One check on the outcome of this process is that the average of the divisional βs (weighted by the value of the divisions) should equal the overall β of the company.

This is a widely used technique. It can certainly add value, although it will often be found that the required returns for the different divisions are not far apart – often within 1 per cent of each other.

Project classifications

The basic character of a project can give a good indication of its level of risk. Cost-reduction projects tend to be low risk. Projects that involve growing the company's revenue stream are riskier. Incorporating this insight in a practical way is not easy. There is a lack of good quantitative evidence on the size of adjustment that is appropriate. However, a schedule that seems intuitively plausible and which is practical and simple to use is as follows. The technique assumes that an overall required return for the company has already been calculated.

Table 4.1

Project category	Adjustment to required return %
Reduction of fixed costs	−3
Reduction of variable costs	−1
Acquisition of similar company	0
Capacity expansion	+1
Introduction of new product or entry to new market	+3 or more

Systems of this type are widely used, although they are perhaps not so common as a divisional approach. 'Project category' adjustments tend to be larger than general 'divisional' adjustments and probably add more value to the appraisal process.

Project analysis method

This technique requires the following.

- The 'Asset β' for the industry (β_I). This is simply the average of the 'Asset βs' for a set of companies which specialise in the relevant line of business.
- The Revenue Sensitivity of the project (S_R). This is defined as the percentage rise/fall in the revenue of this project that would be associated with a 1 per cent rise/fall in the revenue of the industry.
- The Operational Gearing of the project relative to the industry. Operational gearing refers to the percentage change in operating revenue that results from a 1 per cent change in sales. Operating revenue (OR) is cash flow before the subtraction of interest and depreciation. Operational gearing is, in effect, a measure of the relative importance of fixed (in relation to output) costs (FC) in the financial structure of the project. Specifically, it can be shown that the operational gearing of the project (G_p) is defined as:

$$G_p = (OR + FC)OR$$

The values of OR and FC may vary from year to year, in which case the present values of these two quantities over the project life should be used.

The operational gearing of the industry is defined similarly. The 'Project β' (β_P) can then be calculated as

$$\beta_P = \beta_I \times S_R \times \frac{G_P}{G_I}$$

The β_P is then converted directly into a required rate of return using the CAPM formula. This is not an easy formula to apply accurately, and it may be necessary to make rough estimates of the numbers required.

Nevertheless, this method does a good job of focusing attention on features of a project that will add or reduce risk and showing how the required return can be adapted accordingly.

Consider a car manufacturer planning to manufacture a new, luxury sports car. How should the required return for this project vary from the rate generally used in car manufacturing projects?

Sales of luxury cars are more volatile over the economic cycle than sales of their humbler brethren. So S_R for this project will be greater than 1 and will tend to push the required return up.

If conventional manufacturing techniques are used, the operational gearing of this project will probably match the industry average. If, however, the decision was made to use composite construction rather than steel for the body, and to subcontract the body manufacture to a composite specialist, this would, substantially reduce annual fixed costs for space, equipment, etc. The change would justify a lower required return in the analysis of the project.

CONCLUSIONS

The required return on capital should be related to the risk to which the capital is exposed. This chapter has looked at the various ways in which this precept can be put into practice.

Managers have a choice of method. More technically accurate methods are more complex to use. Many companies will opt for the simple solution of using one rate for all projects. This chapter has shown how such a rate can be calculated, adjusted to the different cash flow definitions that may be used.

The second part of the chapter showed how a rate can be tailored to the specific characteristics of a project. One simple adjustment can adjust the rate to the industry in which the project is located, where the company's operations span more than one industry. Another adjustment can reflect the project character. Cost saving projects are less risky than proposed expansion. Finally, the chapter explained a method of measuring the risk of individual projects, which is more sophisticated but still capable of being used in practice.

NPV techniques

INTRODUCTION

We have seen that project cash flow can be defined in several different ways. We have also shown how risk-adjusted required returns can be set. This chapter brings these two elements together to generate an NPV for the project. But, as in so many cases in this briefing, the job is not as simple as it may initially seem and there is more than one way of doing it.

To illustrate the different methods, we shall first set out a brief example.

Tingle plc is planning to take advantage of current interest in astrology to produce knitwear with zodiac patterns incorporated. Operating revenue is expected to be £120,000 per year for three years. New equipment costing £240,000 is needed, which can be written off for tax purposes on a straight line basis over three years, at which time the product will be withdrawn. Tingle will borrow £100,000 in connection with this project at 11 per cent. £30,000 of debt will be repaid in each of the first two years and £40,000 in the final year. (So the interest payments are 11% × £100,000 = £11,000 in the first year; 11% × £70,000 = £7,700 in the second year etc.).

The corporate tax rate is 35 per cent. This is a typical project for Tingle. Its equity β is 1.20 and the ERP is believed to be 7 per cent. The risk-free rate is 11 per cent. From this, it can be calculated that the 'Asset β' is

$$\frac{E}{E + D(1 - T)}\, \beta_E = \frac{140,000}{140,000 + 65,000}(1.20) = 0.82$$

The schedule of cash flows is as follows.

Table 5.1 Schedule of cash flows

	0	1	2	3
Operating revenues	(240,000)	120,000	120,000	120,000
Full tax charge		(14,000)	(14,000)	(14,000)
Cash flow	(240,000)	106,000	106,000	106,000
Boundary 1				
Tax subsidy		3,850	2,695	1,540
Cash flow	(240,000)	109,850	108,695	107,540
Boundary 2				
Cash flows to debtholders	100,000	(41,000)	(37,700)	(44,400)
Cash flow to shareholders	(140,000)	68,850	70,995	63,140
Boundary 3				

Calculating the NPV from these cash flows can be done in several ways. In this example the cost of debt is 11 per cent, and the cost of equity to Tingle, using CAPM, is

$$\text{Required return} = \text{Risk-free rate} + (\text{Equity } \beta \times \text{ERP})$$
$$= 11\% + (1.20 \times 7\%)$$
$$= 19.4\%$$

WEIGHTED AVERAGE COST OF CAPITAL

Weighted Average Cost of Capital (WACC) is a traditional method. It has been taught for a long time and is probably the most widely used approach. With this technique:

- the cash flows are measured at boundary 1, i.e. they ignore the tax subsidy

- the tax subsidy is included in the analysis by a reduction in the cost of debt. In this example the cost of debt is Kd = 11%, but the 'after-tax' cost is Kd (1 − T) = 11%(1 − 0.35) = 7.15%.

This debt rate is used in the calculation of the weighted average cost of capital. So the required rate is

(Proportion of equity finance × Cost of equity) + (Proportion of debt finance × After-tax cost of debt)

$$(\frac{140,000}{240,000} \times 0.194) + (\frac{100,000}{240,000} \times 0.0715)$$

$$= 0.1430 \text{ or } 14.30\%$$

In this example, the debt/equity mix for financing the individual project is given. Often, however, no specific information is available, and the proportions of equity and debt used in the formula will simply be the target proportions for the whole company.

The rate calculated in this way is known as the weighted average cost of capital or WACC. Discounting the boundary 1 cash flows at this rate gives

$$\text{NPV}_{\text{WACC}} = -240,000 + \frac{106,000}{1.1430} + \frac{106,000}{(1.1430)^2} + \frac{106,000}{(1.1430)^3}$$

$$= 4,859$$

The WACC approach is a simple and popular method. However, it is important to note that it follows a rather convoluted logic. The cash flows are not the cash flows that the company will actually receive (because the 'tax subsidy' is excluded) and the required return is not the risk-adjusted return for the cash flows being appraised (which would be found using the CAPM formula and the 'Asset β' of 0.82). Instead the method relies on 'offsetting errors'. The tax subsidy is removed from the cash flows and incorporated into the required returns and, in general, the results are entirely satisfactory.

But it can cause confusion. Consider the following example. In the US, Delta Airlines is profitable but Eastern Airlines is not. Eastern pays no corporate tax (its T = 0), so its after-tax cost of debt is equal to the pre-tax cost and, with all other factors equal, Delta has a lower weighted average cost of capital than Eastern. 'Unfair' cries Eastern. 'We are a struggling airline. Why should the tax system operate to disadvantage us on financing costs relative to our more prosperous rival?'

This argument is nonsense. In its calculations, Eastern will receive higher cash flows (because no tax is subtracted) which more than compensates for the higher required return. But the story illustrates the confusion that can be created by WACC's 'offsetting errors' approach.

ADJUSTED PRESENT VALUE

The Adjusted Present Value (APV) technique also uses the 'boundary 1' cash flows, and it discounts them at the appropriate rate for the projects 'Asset β'. The boundary 1 cash flows do not include the tax subsidies. With the APV method, these are evaluated separately and added-in to the NPV value.

In the Tingle example, the Asset β is 0.82 and the required return for this level of risk, using CAPM, is

$$\text{Required return} = \text{Risk-free rate} + (\beta \times \text{ERP})$$
$$= 11\% + (0.82 \times 7\%)$$
$$= 16.74\%$$

and the present value of the boundary 1 cash flows is

$$\text{NPV(boundary 1)} = -240{,}000 + \frac{106{,}000}{1.1674} + \frac{106{,}000}{(1.1674)^2} + \frac{106{,}000}{(1.1674)^3}$$

$$= -4{,}794$$

We now value the tax subsidy payments. We assume that the company is, and will remain, in a taxpaying position. In this case the payments are risk-free and should be discounted at the risk-free (debt) rate of 11 per cent. This gives

$$NPV(\text{Tax subsidy}) = \frac{3,850}{1.11} + \frac{2,695}{(1.11)^2} + \frac{1,540}{(1.11)^3}$$

$$= 6,782$$

Using this method, the total NPV of the project is calculated as

$$NPV_{APV} = -4,794 + 6,782 = 1,988$$

Note that the 'Asset β' could have been calculated to reflect the risk of the specific project (e.g. by deriving a 'Project β' as described in Chapter 4. APV can easily accommodate this additional refinement.

WACC VERSUS APV

NPVs calculated by these two methods are not the same. The WACC methodology contains the implicit assumption that the debt/equity ratio of finance for the project remains constant throughout its life. Where the debt/equity ratio being used is, for simplicity, the debt/equity target for the overall company, this is a very reasonable assumption.

The two NPVs look very different. NPV_{WACC} is larger than NPV_{APV}. But in relation to the overall size of the project, the difference is not very great; less than 1 per cent of the initial outlay on the project. This degree of accuracy would usually be regarded as very good in a project appraisal context. Inaccuracies in the cash flow measurement process will generally outweigh inaccuracies in the NPV methodology.

APV has one notable advantage. It isolates and values separately the financing benefits associated with the project. These financing benefits can come in a variety of forms – deductability of interest payments, deductability of lease payments, subsidised interest rates that are available for investing in disadvantaged regions, 'launch aid' for new civil aircraft programmes, etc.

This is useful, partly because it can help the decision-makers to see where the NPV is coming from. Is the underlying project profitable or is all the gain coming from the financial deal with which it is packaged? More specifically, there may be many different variants of the same project under review, differing in size, location, timescale, etc. The set of managers working on the financing package may be different from the set of managers working on the other aspects of the project. The APV method will measure separately the success of these two groups in structuring the project to give maximum NPV.

OTHER METHODS OF APPRAISAL

Equity cash flows

Shareholders take any profit – and any loss. They receive the NPV of any project. The NPV of the cash flows to and from the debtholders will be zero. The NPV of a project can be correctly measured using simply the equity cash flows.

Equity cash flows must be discounted at an equity required return. In the Tingle example, the β_E of 1.20 gives a required return

$$\text{Risk-free rate} + (\beta_E \times \text{ERP})$$

$$= 11\% + (1.20 \times 7\%)$$

and the NPV of the shareholders' cash flows is

$$\text{NPV(Equity flows)} = (140,000) + \frac{68,850}{1.194} + \frac{70,995}{(1.194)^2} + \frac{63,140}{(1.194)^3}$$

$$= 4,555$$

It may seem appropriate in private companies to use this approach. How much must the controlling family put in and how much will they get back? It can also be appropriate for investment analysts or investment managers, who are deciding whether to support a major project by a company in which they are shareholders.

The 'overall' rate method

The 'overall' rate method uses the 'boundary 2' cash flows, i.e. company cash flows including the tax subsidy and any other side-effects of the financing method. If the tax subsidy is put into the cash flows, it does not need to be allowed for in the required return. So these cash flows should be discounted at *a* weighted average cost of debt and equity, but the formula is not quite the same as *the* WACC. The pre-tax cost of debt is used, giving the formula

$$\frac{E}{D+E}.K_e + \frac{D}{D+E}.K_d$$

which in the case of the Tingle example is

$$[\frac{140,000}{240,000} \times 0.194] + [\frac{100,000}{240,000} \times 0.11] = 0.159 \text{ or } 15.9\%$$

Giving an NPV with the boundary 2 cash flows of

$$NPV_{B2} = 240{,}000 + \frac{109{,}850}{1.159} + \frac{108{,}695}{(1.159)^2} + \frac{107{,}540}{(1.159)^3}$$

$$= 4{,}772$$

CONCLUSIONS

This chapter has looked at different ways of calculating NPV.

Weighted Average Cost of Capital (WACC)

The advantages of this method are as follows.

- Simplicity. The individual carrying out the appraisal does not require information about how the project will be financed.

- It is fully accurate when the project is 'typical' of the company's activities and is financed from the company's general pool of capital.

- Even when these conditions are not fully met, WACC is attractive as an uncomplicated system that is probably as accurate as the cash flow estimates will allow.

Adjusted Present Value (APV)

This is a more complex, sophisticated and potentially more accurate method.

- APV requires specific information on the financing package which will fund the project.

- APV allows the use of a 'project-specific' required rate of return. This can be useful if the risk characteristic of the project is significantly different from the corporate average.

- APV breaks down the NPV into the contribution of the underlying project and the contribution of the associated financial package. This breakdown can be helpful in trimming and adjusting the project into an optimal format.

The chapter also looked briefly at NPV assessment using equity cash flows and using the cash flows including tax subsidy. These are both workable methods, but they have not proved as popular as WACC and APV.

Risk analysis

INTRODUCTION

This chapter will explain Sensitivity Analysis and Monte Carlo Simulation, the two key techniques of risk analysis.

Risk has already been incorporated into the appraisal process by using a risk-adjusted return. So why do we need to return to this topic? The main reasons are

- analysis based on expected values only may give a misleading picture
- if the overall risk and the sources of that risk can be identified, management may wish to modify the project to change the risk profile.

Risk in a project should not be treated as a 'given' factor, outside management control. Modern finance strongly pushes the idea that risk can be measured and that various management policies can be used to reduce it or to offload it onto another party.

Sensitivity Analysis

Sensitivity Analysis is a way of identifying where the main risks in the project are coming from. Having identified the risk-sources, management can then consider whether they should be reduced. One way of reducing risk is to postpone the project and undertake further market or technical research.

It is not management's job to get rid of as much risk as possible. The market in risk is generally a pretty efficient one. Offloading risk will usually involve offloading some of the return as well. So management should only be looking to pass risk on to another party when there is some reason to believe that the other party can bear the risk at lower cost, or can do more to control the risk.

If the project involves buying new aircraft, who should bear the risk that the fuel efficiency of the engines falls below specification or that the engines should need overhaul more frequently than planned? Surely the engine manufacturer. Put it in the contract. If a car rental company needs more cars, who should bear the risk relating to the value on disposal? The manufacturer? After all, it controls advertising, production and new price levels. Put a guaranteed disposal price in the contract. Sensitivity Analysis is a method of identifying the substantial elements of risk in the project that might be strong candidates for transfer elsewhere.

Monte Carlo Simulation

The technique of looking at overall project risk – which is likely to involve the interaction of the different risk elements – is termed Monte Carlo Simulation. Monte Carlo Simulation adds value in three ways.

- The expected NPV of the project may not be the same as the NPV calculated using the expected value of each risky factor. This sounds paradoxical but the difference between NPVs calculated in these two ways can be significant. Simulation, for example, might demonstrate that the losses when the risk variables fall short of expectation are much larger than the gains if they are above expectation. A conventional NPV calculation will not reveal this, and can therefore be misleading.

- Large losses from a project may push a company into financial distress and prevent it from accepting good investment opportunities in the future. This can be very damaging to shareholder value. Simulation will show the overall distribution of possible project outcomes and will help to identify the probability of an outcome leading to financial distress. This may influence the decision to accept or reject.

- Inspection of the range of possible outcomes will indicate opportunities to enhance the project by adapting it to prevailing circumstances. These may be opportunities to abandon the project rather than continue for a long period in difficult circumstances. There may be opportunities to scale up if things turn out well.

Sensitivity Analysis and Monte Carlo Simulation will both be illustrated through a single example.

Modern Ceramics plc

Modern Ceramics specialises in producing very high quality ceramics to designs by leading potters in Europe and Japan. It is considering putting on the market a limited edition of 800 painted and glazed ceramic plates to a set of designs by a well-known artist, Derek Hawkney. Each plate approved by Mr Hawkney would be signed and numbered. Mr Hawkney is known to be a perfectionist and it is possible that a significant number of plates (estimated at 20 per cent of production) will fail his appraisal and be scrapped.

Mr Hawkney and his dealer are very anxious that the Hawkney name is not associated with 'sales or discounts'. The price of US$800, fixed firmly in dollars, will be the proceeds to Modern Ceramics (after gallery commissions). The exchange rate is $1.60 = £1.00. Any plates not sold at full price must be destroyed at the end of five years. As long as plates remain on sale, an annual promotion budget of £30,000 will be spent in ways approved by Mr Hawkney. Modern Ceramics expects that its marketing programme will sell the plates at a steady rate and estimates that they will all be sold in three years. The production cost is £190 per plate with stockholding costs of £35 per year for unsold plates. Tax is ignored in this example. On the basis of these expected value numbers, and a required return of 15 per cent, the NPV of this project is £34,036.

SENSITIVITY ANALYSIS

We are going to carry out Sensitivity Analysis on this project to identify the key risk sources and to consider whether, and how, they should be controlled.

The risk factors

We shall consider three risk sources in this project:

- the sales rate
- the exchange rate
- the scrappage rate.

Figures 6.1, 6.2, and 6.3 show how NPV will vary with each of these variables. Note that Sensitivity Analysis is a 'one-variable-at-a-time' procedure. As one factor varies, the others are held at their expected value.

The information needed

It is sometimes recommended that Sensitivity Analysis should consider the consequences of each risk element moving 10 per cent from its expected value. This is not helpful. There may be risk elements which we are confident will not vary by more than 1 or 2 per cent from their expected value. Sensitivity Analysis needs to consider how risky each element is. This means that extra information is needed compared to a straight NPV calculation.

The information needed is a set of 'bounds' for each factor. For any factor, the '10 per cent upper bound' is a value so high that there is only a 10 per cent chance that it will be exceeded. The 10 per cent lower bound is defined similarly. Suppose in the Modern Ceramics' example, the bounds are:

	Lower Bound	Upper Bound
Sales rate	150	450
Exchange rate	1.30	1.90
Scrappage rate	10%	30%

These bounds are shown in Figures 6.1, 6.2 and 6.3. The prospect of values outside the bounds are generally de-emphasized in Sensitivity Analysis (note, there is a 20 per cent chance of this occurring). The focus is on the 'danger triangle' showing the outcomes that give a negative NPV. We have drawn the diagrams to the same scale and so, in a very rough way, the size of the danger triangle is an indication of the amount of risk arising from a particular factor. In our diagrams it is clear that sales is the main source of risk with exchange rate coming second; scrappage has no danger triangle at all.

Fig. 6.1

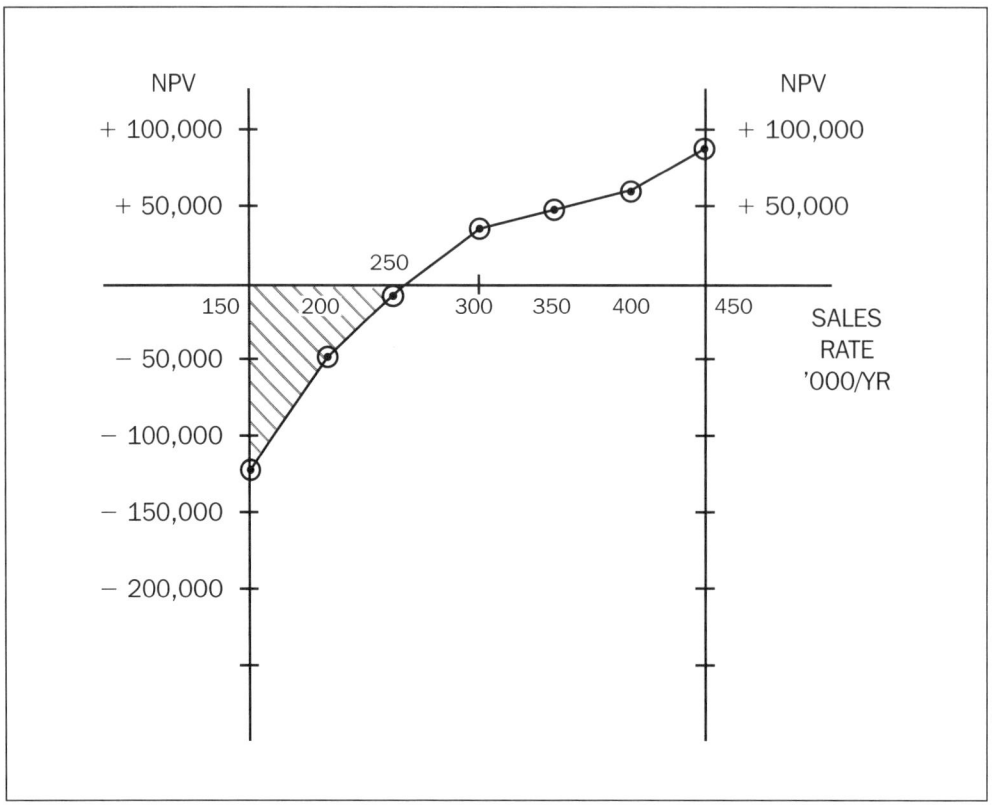

Fig. 6.2

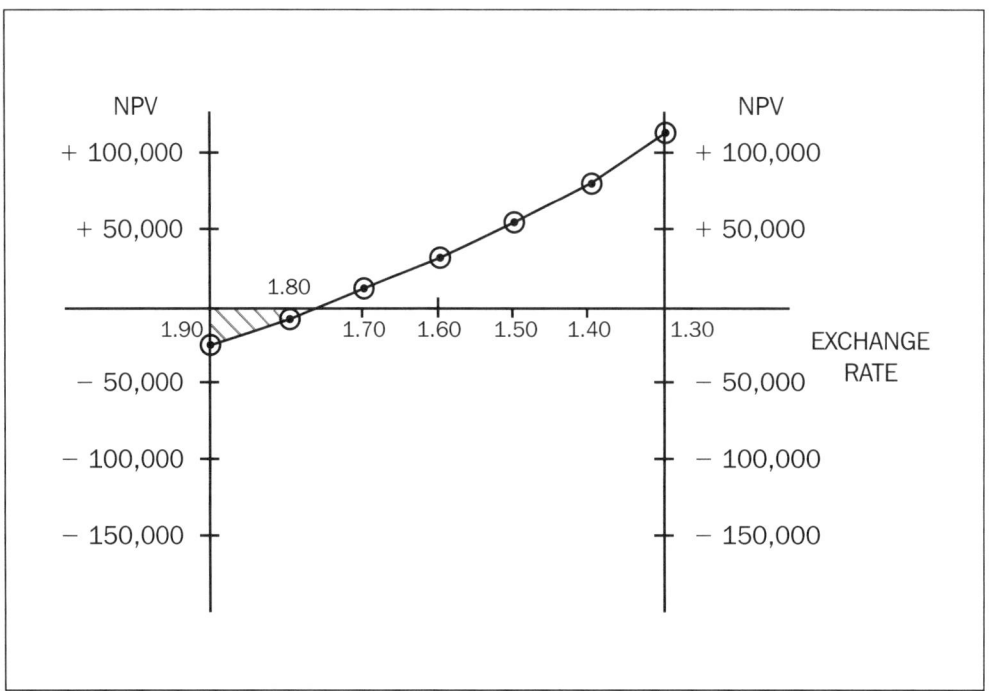

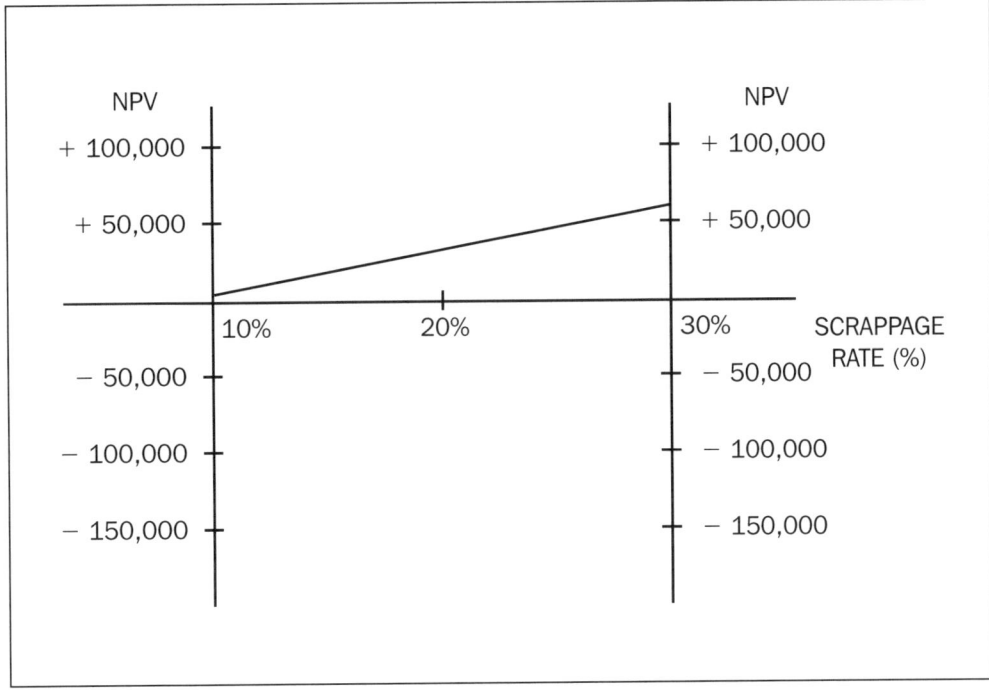

Fig. 6.3

Where do 'bounds' come from?

When data is collected for a project, everyone involved knows that some of the estimates are risky or uncertain. When managers are asked for a point estimate, the information that they possess about the spread of possible outcomes is suppressed. If management is asked to set bounds – 'Give me a cost for this new building that you are 90 per cent sure will not be exceeded' – they can generally give a number. If they have a probability distribution at the back of their minds, it is no more difficult to give the 10th percentile than the 50th. Some bounds may be scientifically based. Others may be mere guesstimates. But they are still likely to contain valuable information for appraisal purposes.

Note that bound estimates may be biased. Ask a group of managers or students – 'How many take-offs and landings were there last year at Gatwick airport?' and then ask for 10 per cent upper and lower bounds. It will be found that the true answer lies outside the bounds in about half the cases. This follows a general law of human psychology. People think they know more than they actually do. Even if you have not studied psychology you may have observed this law at work in your business experience. It may be appropriate to widen the bounds before carrying out risk analysis to compensate for this effect. If managers' estimates can and will be checked against the subsequent outcome, this is another antidote to overconfident estimation.

Using Sensitivity Analysis

With the major risk sources identified, the next question is whether any of them can be conveniently limited or off-loaded.

General methods of risk control

Some risks can be handled by insurance (will it rain on an outdoor event?). Some can be off-loaded onto suppliers (instead of buying trains, buy 'train services' and ensure that repair and maintenance costs fall on the supplier). Raw material prices can be hedged in commodity markets. Credit risks on export transactions can often be passed to Government Agencies. It may be possible to sign up customers (for an electricity plant, for example) to a long-term purchase contract with minimum volumes. Any risk can sometimes be reduced by further market or technical research. We will give further consideration to risk control techniques in the context of the Modern Ceramics example.

For Modern Ceramics the Sensitivity Analysis has shown a large danger triangle for the sales rate; a small danger triangle for the exchange rate and no danger triangle at all for the scrappage rate. So the analysis is telling us to focus most strongly on the sales rate risk. Although it is highly likely that all the plates will be sold within the five-year contract period, it still makes a major difference whether the goods can be sold quickly. Slow sales will incur large costs of storage and continued marketing. What creative ideas can Modern Ceramics come up with to kick-start sales? Negotiate a front-loading of the marketing budget? Sponsor a Hawkney exhibition to coincide with the launch? Personal signing sessions by the artist?

Exchange rate risk is also significant. There are several hedging techniques which lie outside the scope of this briefing. Different methods of arranging a financial hedge have been mentioned already. Note that exchange exposure, commodity price exposure and interest rate exposure need to be viewed on a company-wide basis. The Hawkney project puts Modern Ceramics 'long' of dollars. There might be other parts of its activities that put it 'short' – perhaps Modern Ceramics imports ovens from the US for sale to amateur potters in Britain. In this case the Hawkney project will act as a natural hedge for its existing activities. Alternatively, Modern Ceramics might be able to restructure the current deal to get a better currency hedge. If Modern Ceramics could arrange that its annual marketing commitment was the equivalent of $50,000 rather than £30,000, the exposure could be substantially reduced. But if no such natural or 'internal' hedges are available, the markets will give opportunities for a financial hedge.

Sensitivity Analysis has shown that scrappage risk is not a significant danger to the success of the project. Any ways of reducing the expected number of scrapped plates would be useful, but the need to control the risk – to narrow the bounds – is not a high priority issue.

MONTE CARLO SIMULATION

To get an overall picture of project risk, all the risk elements must be considered simultaneously. To do this, more information is needed:

- the full probability distributions of the risky elements
- the linkages between the elements.

Where relevant, you may also need to know the amount that the company can lose before the losses have a negative impact on the rest of the company's business.

Probability distributions

It is possible to go beyond asking for the 10th, 50th and 90th points of the distribution and ask for a full probability distribution. Such a distribution might be expressed as follows:

Probability	Exchange rate
0.05	1.20
0.10	1.40
0.20	1.50
0.30	1.60
0.20	1.70
0.10	1.80
0.05	2.00

For this to be a proper probability distribution, all the probabilities must add to one.

A simpler approach, which uses the 'bounds' and does not require asking any further questions, is to assume that the probability distributions of the individual risk elements are normal. The 10 per cent upper bound is approximately 1.3 standard deviations from the mean. So, assuming normality, if the expected exchange rate is \$1.60 = £1.00 and the upper bound is \$1.90 = £1.00, the standard deviation is

$$(\$1.90 - \$1.60)1.3 = \$0.30/1.3 = \$0.23$$

Linkage between the elements

Consider the house-building industry. It is a risky business. Firms will be uncertain how many houses they can sell, what price they can sell them at and what financing charges they will face for unsold houses and undeveloped land. An additional problem is that all these variables tend to move together. In the UK economy, interest rates are sometimes raised to protect the pound and ward off inflation. As a side effect, they depress economic growth. So house builders find that they cannot sell houses because mortgage rates are high and potential buyers feel insecure in their jobs. House prices fall. And interest rises on larger-than-expected stocks complete the triple whammy. When the links between the different risk elements are taken into account, house building stands out as a high-risk activity. This is a general truth. Linkage between the different risk elements is often very important in determining the overall risk level.

In the Modern Ceramics example, the sales rate is likely to be linked to the exchange rate. The price is fixed in dollars. Most Hawkney fans are in the US, but not all. If the dollar falls, the price in pounds will fall and British Hawkney fans will be encouraged to buy. This might ameliorate the effects of a weak dollar. This helpful interaction should be taken into account when analysing the overall risk of the project.

The risk limit

One major benefit of Monte Carlo Simulation arises with large projects which have the potential, if they go wrong, to create financial distress for the company as a whole. Financial distress does not mean bankruptcy, although that might occur in an extreme case. Financial distress is simply a state in which the company is forced to watch its cash flow to such an extent that it operates inefficiently and/or has to pass up on good investment opportunities. If the capital markets are perfect, financial distress will not arise. As far as giant multinationals are concerned, access to capital is nearly perfect and prospects of financial distress are remote. But smaller and medium-sized companies may need to consider this eventuality. How much can we lose on a project before it starts to damage the rest of the company? Suppose that for Modern Ceramics this amount is £100,000.

The output from a simulation

Monte Carlo Simulation involves calculating the project NPV a large number of times. For every NPV, a value for each of the risky factors is drawn from the appropriate probability distribution. If any pair of variables is linked – with one influenced by the other – select the independent variable first. Then modify the value of the dependent variable to reflect the influence of the independent one.

If we calculate 100 NPVs in this way, we shall be able to answer some frequently asked questions. What is the probability that we will lose money on this project? If, out of 100 simulated NPVs, 30 were negative, we would conclude that the probability of a loss is 30 per cent. We can also tell any inquisitive manager the probability that the project will be a big winner and make more than £100,000 by using the same approach.

The simulation procedure

It is not the intention of this briefing to cover spreadsheet analysis. But many analysts do not realise that Monte Carlo Simulation is a very simple process using spreadsheet functions, and we shall cover the necessary techniques briefly.

Generating risk variables

There are two main ways of doing this. If we have a discrete probability distribution – say the exchange rate distribution above – then the variable can be simulated using a lookup table. If we set out the table as follows:

Row/Column	A	B
1	0	1.20
2	5	1.40
3	15	1.50
4	35	1.60
5	65	1.70
6	85	1.80
7	95	2.00
8	100	

Then, in any cell (say A10) we generate a two-digit random number. In the cell where we want a randomly generated exchange rate, the Excel command would be:

@Vlookup(A10, A1:A7)

In words, look up the number that corresponds to A10 in the table where the left-hand column runs from A1 to A7. If the randomly generated number at A10 had been 22, the spreadsheet would move down column A until it reached a number greater than 22 (it would reach 35 in cell A4). It would then go back (to 15 in cell A3) and read the number from the adjacent column (1.50 in B3). This process gives a 5 per cent chance of generating a $1.20 exchange rate, a 10 per cent chance of generating $1.40 and so on, just as we require.

An alternative method is to use the random number generator. Excel offers several distributions (In the 'Data Analysis' part of 'Tools'). The spreadsheet can be asked directly to generate an exchange rate number from a normal distribution with a mean of 1.60 and a standard deviation of 0.23.

Interaction between variables

In the Modern Ceramics example, a lower value for the dollar would tend to increase the sales rate. Suppose we believed that every 10c fall in the exchange rate would increase sales by 20 per year. In this case we could:

- generate the exchange rate
- generate unadjusted sales
- calculate the sales variable as

$$\text{Unadjusted sales} + (\text{Exchange rate} - 1.60)\ \frac{20}{0.10}$$

This inter-relationship is assumed in the simulation graph Figure 6.4.

Calculate NPV

Excel calculates the present value of a sequence of cash flows in A1:A10 at an interest rate in A12 with the command

$$@PV[A12, A1:A10]$$

Note that with this command, the first cash flow is discounted [i.e. it is assumed to take place in one year's time]. If A1 was an immediate cash flow, then the formula would be modified to

$$= @PV(A12, A2:A10) + A1$$

Once one NPV has been calculated, the whole procedure can be copied N times (either vertically or horizontally as convenient) to make N simulations of the project. A minimum value for N would be 100. 400 or 1000 are also popular values.

Graphing

The NPV values are then arranged in ascending order using the 'sort' command. An adjacent column is created, starting at 1.00 and descending by steps of 1/N

[Put 1.00 in A1; = A1 − 1/N in A2; and copy down from A2]. This creates the probabilities. Then use an X−Y graph to plot the probabilities against the NPVs.

A graph for the Modern Ceramics problem is shown in Figure 6.4. It has been calculated on the basis of the given upper and lower bounds for the variables and assuming a normal distribution. The assumed interaction between the variables is described above and N has been set at 100.

Fig. 6.4

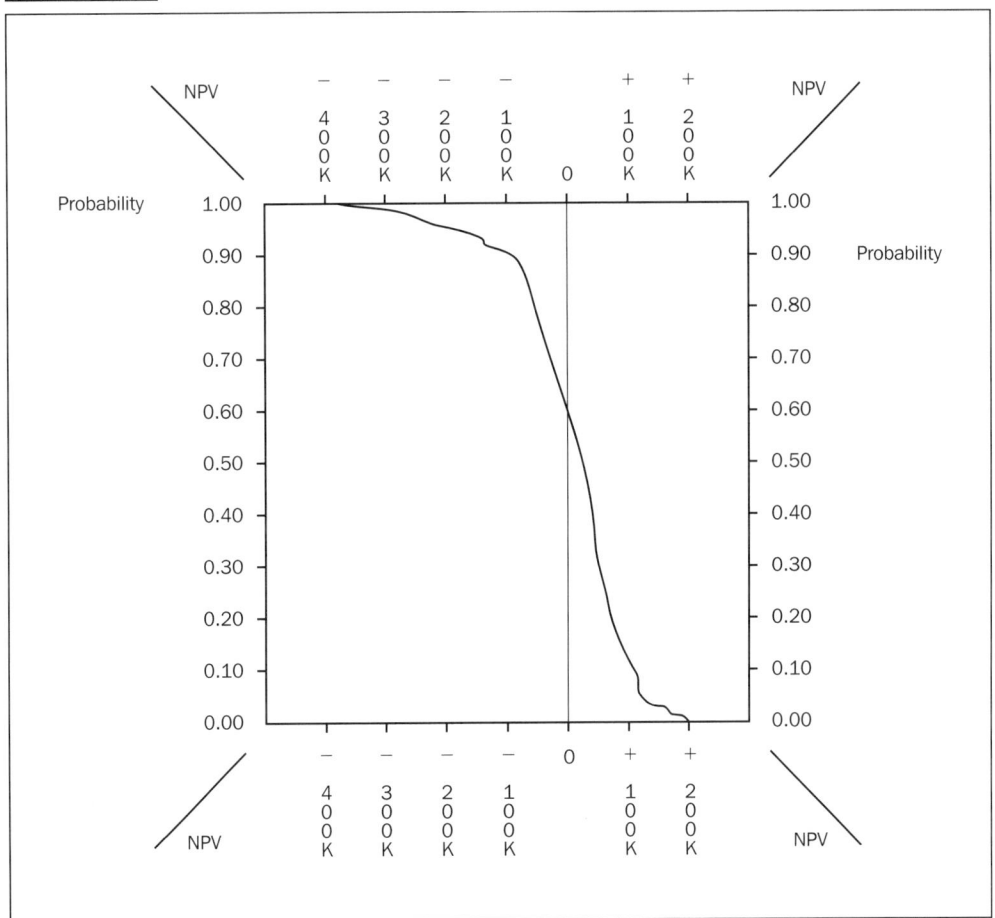

The average of the 100 NPV values from this simulation has been £5,255.

Interpreting the simulation results

In interpreting the graph, it is not appropriate to give much weight to the far tails of the distribution. Although these numbers may catch the eye, the simulation procedure is likely to be highly inaccurate in illustrating the extreme values. The extremes will be very sensitive to the types of distribution assumed [discrete, normal, logical, etc.] and to the exact form of the interaction between the variables.

The simulation procedure has more credibility when indicating the interquartile range [from an NPV of −£41K to an NPV of +£60K in our example], or even the inter-decile range (from the 10th to 90th decile of the simulated NPV; −£95K to +£107K in this case).

We first compare the average of the 100 NPVs from the simulation (£5,255) with the NPV that was originally calculated on expected values (£34,036). There is a significant difference. Our detailed analysis has shown that the downside from worse-than-expected values exceeds the upside from better-than-expected values. The new 'average NPV' is the better indicator of value, so Monte Carlo Simulation has shown us that this project is significantly less attractive than it initially appeared.

The second question is whether Modern Ceramics can comfortably stand the losses indicated at the lower quartile and the lower decile. If so, there is no reason to second-guess the decision based on average NPV. But if not, a reconsideration is necessary. It is unlikely that the full theory of option analysis can be brought to bear on the problem. More likely Modern Ceramics will simply have to consider what is the probability of financial distress being generated by this project and how much could it cost if financial distance did arise? Are these factors large enough to outweigh a positive NPV? Nine per cent of our simulations gave losses greater than £100,000 – the level that would trigger distress.

INTERACTION BETWEEN PROJECTS

Monte Carlo Simulations are careful to incorporate linkages between the different project variables. It is also important to consider how this project will relate to the rest of the company's activities. Consider an accountancy firm deciding whether to develop a specialist insolvency practice. Insolvency business is highly geared to the uncertainties of the economic cycle. Simulation might show the prospect of major losses among the range of outcomes.

However, the insolvency practice is likely to do badly in prosperous times when the rest of the firm's activities are doing well. When it does badly, the losses it makes are likely to be carried comfortably by other departments. Insolvency work may be a natural hedge for the firm's other activities and the picture of the project's risk generated by Monte Carlo Simulation would be incomplete and misleading.

It would be possible to draw up a simulation of the complete set of company activities. Possible – but not common in practice. The interactions between an individual project and the firm as a whole are usually considered but not subjected to formal analysis.

Finance texts will generally explain that diversifying risk is not a proper objective for companies. Investors diversify and company management should concentrate on finding good investments whenever they can – which may be a specialised niche defined by the firm's comparative advantage.

This is generally a good argument – but not always. We return to the issue of financial distress. If one project goes wrong, opportunities to accept good projects in the future may be lost. So interactions between projects may need to be considered.

EXTENDING THE ANALYSIS: REAL OPTIONS

Investment is not a single-period game – decide and forget. Once an investment has been made, new information will be received and 'course corrections' of various types may be needed. Traditionally, this situation was pictured by a decision tree as shown in Figure 6.5.

Fig. 6.5   A decision tree

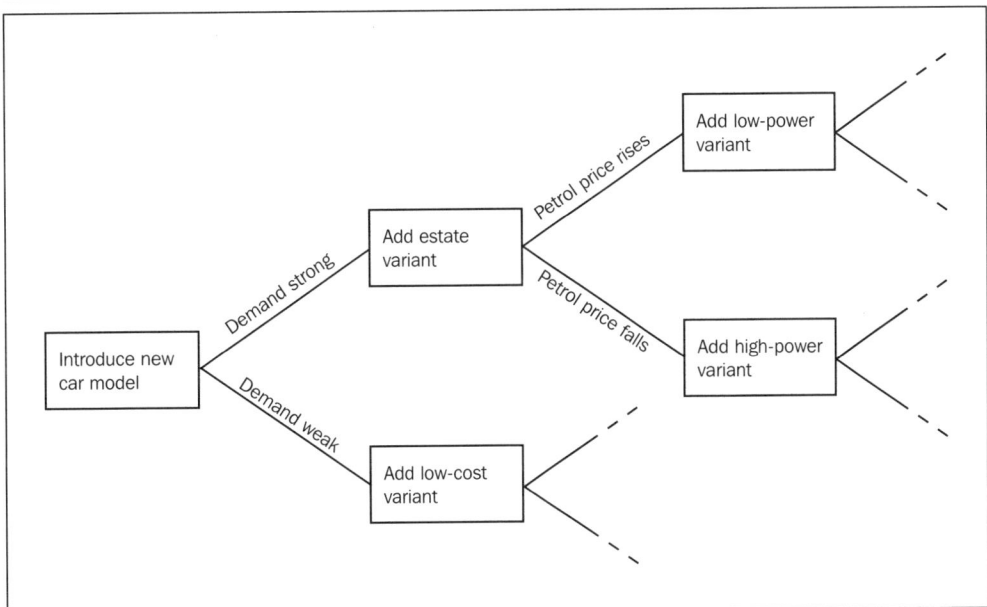

The company makes a decision; events take place in the business environment; the company responds with a new decision and the cycle repeats. If the probabilities of the different future events can be estimated, the optimum initial move in this chess game can be calculated.

The currently fashionable way to describe this situation is to say that companies have 'options' to review and change their original decisions. These are called 'real options'. This distinguishes them from 'financial options' which relate to financial assets like shares and currencies. As the introduction to this briefing explained, a large part of stock market value is derived from these real options. An investment often brings with it a set of valuable real options. In other cases, an investment may destroy real options. Consideration of the real option dimension is an extremely important aspect of project appraisal. It is often ignored, partly because of the difficulty in estimating option value. But a poor estimate is more useful than no estimate at all.

Options come in many forms, some of which occur regularly.

Abandonment or reversibility

Managers can learn a great deal about investment appraisal from university dons. They can also learn from Mafia dons. Smart criminals with powerful enemies are careful to check the exits from a building before they go in. It is sensible to do the same with investments. If things go wrong, how can you get out?

Calculation of NPV using expected values ignores this issue. It does not distinguish between a 'reversible' investment (where the investment assets can readily be resold) and irreversible ones. But the availability of an abandonment option can greatly reduce the downside risks of a project.

Consider the Modern Ceramics example. The simulation shows possible outcomes in which the negative NPV exceeds the entire cost of making the plates. That is because the model has assumed that no matter how poor the level of sales or how adverse the exchange rate, Modern Ceramics will press on for the full five years of the contact.

This is not sensible. If sales are so low that not even marketing costs can be covered, the plates should be destroyed and the project should be abandoned immediately. Even if sales exceed this level, it may be clear that not all the plates will be sold and some should be scrapped immediately to avoid storage costs.

As well as identifying abandonment options that are already implicit in the project, it is also worth considering whether the project can be restructured to build in more attractive exit opportunities. Mr Hawkney is legitimately concerned that his plates do not appear in shop windows with '50 per cent off' signs. But would he be willing for surplus plates to be sold at a discount to five-star hotels to decorate their suites? Modern Ceramics might be able to establish that a major hotel chain would be prepared to buy on this basis. This would make no difference to the point estimate NPV, but if it capped potential losses at −£100,000, the average NPV from the project would rise to £16,061.

If sufficient information is available, optional abandonment strategies can be calculated mathematically. Often the available information is too limited for these techniques to be used effectively, but interested readers can seek out more advanced texts on this subject.

Postponement

Some projects disappear tomorrow if they are not accepted today – acquisition opportunities for example – but many can be postponed. This can be looked at in an options framework, but in a slightly indirect way. The ability to carry out the investment is a valuable option. If the investment is carried out today, the options to do it in the future are effectively thrown away or killed. So the decision rule for undertaking a postponable investment is not

$$NPV_{\text{accept today}} > 0 \text{ but}$$

$$NPV_{\text{accept today}} - \text{Value of option to invest in the future} > 0.$$

Postponement is valuable because new facts or information may arrive which make the project unattractive. So, by postponing, there is a chance that you will avoid making a mistake.

As a simple example, suppose a zero discount rate and zero risk aversion. A project, if accepted today, has $NPV_0 = £5$ million. If the project is delayed one period, it is equally likely that the NPV will be

$$NPV_{1A} = -£12m \qquad NPV_{1B} = £4m \qquad NPV_{1C} = £20m.$$

The average of these three is £4m so, if we were to proceed in ignorance of which state will occur (A, B or C), it is more profitable to accept the project immediately than to opt for a delayed launch.

However, we can do better than ignorance. If we wait until period 1 we can see if state A has arisen and, if so, pull the project. The value of the option to make the decision at T = 1 is

$$£4m/3 + £20m/3 = £8m$$

So should we invest in T = 0? No, because

$$NPV_0 - \text{Value of option to invest at T = 1}$$

$$= £5m - £8m = -£3$$

This is negative. We should delay. In general terms the value of the option to invest in the future will be linked to the amount of change in the project variables which can be expected over the next time period. The bigger the risks, the greater the likelihood that you will regret having launched the project today and the greater the value of the option. We shall return to this 'options paradox'. In general a project with riskier cash flows is less attractive. But a riskier investment environment tends to make an option worth more.

Expand

If a project is going badly – how can we get out? If a project goes well – how can we build on that success? If a new restaurant works well in London, can it be rolled out in the provinces? Internationally? Can it spawn cookery books and videos? Can its brand be extended to chilled supermarket dishes?

If a project carries large expansion options such as these, it can be worthwhile proceeding even if the project itself is expected to have a negative NPV. The project should be accepted as long as

$$NPV_{today} + \text{Value of associated future expansion options} > 0$$

Cut the losses: ride the winners. A small proportion of a company's projects will turn out to generate most of the value.

It may be necessary at the beginning of a project to take some action to protect the upside potential. If you are buying ten aircraft for your new, low-fare airline, how much will it cost to sign an option for ten more? If you like their album and are signing a new act for your record label, should you take an option for their next six albums? If you are building a greenfield factory, can you get an option on the next field?

HIDDEN OPTIONS

Abandoning, postponing and expanding are obvious possibilities for the future. But some spectacular business successes have come from spotting options which were not obvious to outsiders. Airlines in the US have made a lot of money from developing and marketing reservation systems (or, at least, the first to spot the option did). The reservations business is a lot less cyclical than the airline business itself. Dixons spotted that the ownership of PC World put it in pole position to offer Internet service and Freeserve has become far more valuable than the underlying retailing business. Scottish Power started with a modest internal telephone system with wires running alongside its power lines. It grew this into Thus, a FTSE 100 company. A mail-order retailer has an option to grow a valuable business selling credit information to third parties. Finding hidden options is a key project appraisal skill.

THE VALUE OF OPTIONS

Mathematical models for valuing financial options are well developed. The maths is complex, the theoretical breakthrough involved has been deemed worthy of the Nobel Prize and the formulae are widely used.

A typical financial option might give the holder the right, but not the obligation to buy a share (current market price X) at price E within time period t. The value of such an option is:

- higher – the greater the value of X
- lower – the greater the value of E
- higher – the greater the value of t
- higher – the greater the risk or volatility of the share price X
- higher – the greater the interest rate.

There are considerable differences between real and financial options. In particular, real options do not have the neat, clearly set out, contractual nature of financial options. There are often sets of related options. And the numbers on which to base a formula valuation are often unavailable. Real options are generally valued on a rough-and-ready basis. Consider the following questions.

- 'What is the probability that we will want to exercise this option?'
- 'If the circumstances are right and we do exercise, how much would we expect to make?'

Multiply these two numbers.

But there are valuable insights from the formal option models. An option is generally more valuable the longer its life (t). In 2000, Fiat negotiated an exchange of stock with General Motors. Twenty per cent of Fiat Auto was exchanged for five per cent of GM. But, in addition, Fiat negotiated an option to sell the remaining 80 per cent to GM within a five-year period. The financial terms of this option were not clearly publicised, so the value of the option cannot be estimated. But five years is a long time. The European and global car markets might move from boom to bust in that period. Fiat's option could turn out to be very valuable indeed.

In competitive markets, however, real options often have short lives. If an investment opportunity is not accepted quickly, a competitor may occupy all or part of the market first. He or she may secure 'first mover advantage', and greatly diminish the value of your own option. You cannot always count on being able to postpone.

The other insight from formal option models is that risk makes options more valuable. The riskier the environment the greater the flow of new information and the greater the value of being able to wait and use that information before making a decision. This has introduced a major new perspective to project appraisal. No longer do we think of risk as a purely negative feature of a project – raising the required return and lowering NPV. We now see an additional dimension. Risk brings opportunity.

CONCLUSIONS

This chapter has described the techniques of Sensitivity Analysis and Monte Carlo Simulation and explained how they can be useful to investors. The techniques have been demonstrated through an extended example.

The chapter has stressed the role of options in project appraisal. The value of growth options contributes a very large part of stock market value. It follows that successful project appraisal must take into account the value of options being acquired and options that are being discarded. The chapter discussed how this might be done, while noting that the valuation of real options tends to be a rough and ready process. There is insufficient information available to use standard option pricing formulae.

Specialised appraisal methods

INTRODUCTION

This chapter will cover three 'further topics' in investment appraisal:

- international investment
- replacement decisions
- lease decisions.

INTERNATIONAL INVESTMENT

International investment falls into two distinct categories – investment in developed economies and investment in developing or 'transition' economies. Projects in developed countries pose fewer problems for investment appraisal. It will be possible to use the same techniques as for domestic projects, with minor changes. The key differences will come in three areas; currencies, required return and tax. The principles of cash flow measurement will not be affected, but note that there may be additional management costs, both on-site and at head office, which would not be incurred domestically. The management costs associated with understanding and implementing health and safety legislation, employment law, pension systems, etc., in a new legal environment can be substantial. International projects are also likely to involve a lengthening of the chain of command. All these costs need to be factored in.

Currency issues

Currency risk is not a simple concept. It can be defined in three quite distinct ways.

- **Transaction exposure.** This relates to future commitments to pay or receive foreign currency. Exchange rate risk means that the amounts paid or received, measured in the domestic currency, are uncertain. This risk can be eliminated by hedging in the currency markets, although, as we shall see, there may be no gain from the shareholders' point of view in doing so.

- **Translation exposure.** This is a product of the accounting procedures used for consolidating foreign subsidiary into the accounts of the parent group. The rules are complex and do not always follow economic logic. Suppose a UK parent makes an acquisition in Canada and partly finances the deal with a C$ loan. It would be smart to make such an acquisition before the C$ rises relative to the pound. But this wisdom will not be rewarded in the accounting numbers. The value of the C$ debt liability will be written up, the value of the acquired Canadian business will not, and the accounts will have to incorporate the resulting loss.

Translation exposure is purely a product of financial reporting regulations. It is not a measure of the impact on cash flow or shareholders' wealth. If we could assume that shareholders and other users of accounts could correctly interpret the economic reality underlying the published accounts, then there would be no reason to be concerned with translation exposure at all. Most studies, which have looked at share price reactions to changes in accounting presentation, have concluded that the stock market does a good, rational job in interpreting the figures. It is possible that translation exposure may create problems (for example, it may influence the ratios that are part of the company's borrowing agreements). However, it will generally not be significant in investment appraisal.

■ **Economic exposure.** This is the key measure of currency exposure for appraisal purposes. It measures the sensitivity of shareholders' value to changes in exchange rates. This sensitivity is not always obvious. It may arise in indirect ways.

When Henry Ford decided to buy and develop a Brazilian rubber plantation to produce raw material for tyres – how exposed is this investment to currency fluctuations between the US and Brazil? Hardly at all, surely. The revenues ultimately generated by the project will be in dollars. And, if Brazil is the main source for rubber, currency-related changes in local production costs will be experienced by all competing producers and will tend to be reflected in selling prices. On the other hand, if Mr Ford had set up an assembly operation in Brazil, putting together imported car kits for sale on the local market, the economic exposure would be high. The operation could be squeezed between the dollar cost of the kits and the local currency purchasing power of the market. The risk would be even greater if this assembly plan was competing with fully indigenous or non-US-based assemblers.

Economic exposure can be present in domestically located projects which will involve no foreign currency payments at all. Consider a British business 'Cherry-wood Kitchens', which manufactures high quality kitchen furniture from imported US cherry-wood. It may buy its raw material from the importer in pounds, but the price will reflect the market price of the cherry-wood set, in dollars, in the US market. A rising dollar/pound rate could make Cherry-wood Kitchens less competitive.

Careful analysis may therefore be needed to assess the economic currency exposure associated with an international project – and the same may also be true of domestic projects.

Risk analysis may indicate ways in which the project can be restructured to reduce currency risk. Should loans be taken out in the parent currency or local currency? Can local currency suppliers of inputs be found? Can local managers be used instead of expatriates?

Should exposure be hedged?

It would be a fallacy to believe that investors in UK companies want exposure to sterling and to no other currency. Many such investors will have internationally diversified portfolios. They are quite happy for their shares to be linked to a number of first-world currencies.

But currency risk can be efficiently and cheaply hedged. Even if the benefits are fairly minor, for example, making cash management a more predictable process, it may still be worth doing.

Currency and the appraisal calculation

For an investment project that will be located in a developed economy, the local currency is the natural choice for the appraisal. This will be the easiest way to incorporate local corporate tax payments. The cash flow projections will need to include estimates of local inflation. It will generally not be possible to use the inflation forecasts method described in Chapter 3. Most countries do not have index-linked government bonds. However, economic theory predicts that in the absence of restrictions on capital movements (true in developed economies) real rates will tend to equality across countries. Using the real rate from the UK in the calculation is likely to do a reasonable job of identifying prospective inflation levels. In effect, this approach argues that the inflation premium in Country X compared to the UK is roughly equal to the interest premium in Country X relative to the UK.

Required returns

If cash flows are expressed in foreign currency then so must the required return. The key elements in the required return calculations in Chapter 4 are the risk-free rate and the appropriate premium for risk. We need to consider how these will be affected in an international context.

■ The risk-free rate for the currency in which cash flows have been measured will be directly measurable from the relevant market in government debt.

■ The equity risk premium can be measured directly for the UK, the US and some other 'Anglo-Saxon' economies. The risk premium is in the range 5–8 per cent in most cases. Risk premium in continental Europe cannot be measured over a similarly long time-span due to the scale of disruption in World War II. The evidence for Germany suggests that the risk premium there may be somewhat lower. However, this may be due to the different corporate governance system in Germany. Takeovers are rare in Germany, employees are represented on company boards and share options (which are seen as linking management self-interest with investors rather than employees) are controversial. It is very doubtful whether a risk premium established in such an environment would be relevant for a British or other foreign firm investing in Germany.

Because of the difficulty in measuring the equity risk premium in many countries, and the associated difficulty in using local βs, the recommendation is to use the same risk premium for an international project that would be used for a domestic project of the same character. The suggested methods for tailoring required return to the specific character of a project, discussed in Chapter 4, remain just as relevant in the international context. If the project is a new venture in a new business area, for example, then an additional premium may be justified. But there is nothing in the inherent nature of an international project that makes it more risky than a domestic one.

Tax

A cross-border project will tend to generate a more complex tax situation. In this complexity there is opportunity. Overseas taxes can be minimised by judicious use of transfer pricing, by using substantial local debt (backed, perhaps, by a parent company guarantee), by charging the project royalties for the use of brand names or intellectual property and by various other devices. It may be efficient to use an intermediate subsidiary, based in a third country, to channel project cash in a way that makes best use of tax treaties. In all these matters, nimble and ingenious corporate activities will meet with equally nimble and ingenious responses from tax authorities.

Developing and transition economies

Less developed economies pose a major challenge for international investing companies. It is in the developing world that customers – growing numbers of customers – can be found. About 15 per cent of the global population is in the 'the West' (essentially, Western Europe, North America, Australia and New Zealand) and this proportion is falling. The share of world economic production in the West has fallen from about two-thirds in 1950 to less than one-half. Manufacturing has switched even more strongly to the developing world and to East Asia in particular.

However, the environment for business operations becomes very different once they move into non-western cultures. Western companies which try to establish themselves may suffer rejection.

The provision of electricity to the growing cities and industries of Asia has been described as the world's greatest investment opportunity. In the mid-1990s, agreements were signed to establish Hubco. This organisation, owned by Western companies, would set up a large oil-fired power station in Pakistan, and sell power at an agreed price to WAPCO, the state-owned company involved in electricity distribution. The World Bank was an enthusiastic supporter of the project and assisted in the negotiations. National Power from the UK would be the operator of the plant.

Then the government of Pakistan changed. It announced that Hubco had secured its contract by corruption and that the prices it was charging for electricity were too high. It demanded a reduction. In addition, Western staff were blockaded within their workplace. International management, when they could visit the site, travelled with an armed guard. The clauses in the Hubco agreement which provided for international arbitration of disputes proved ineffective.

Subsequent negotiations, in which Hubco received support from the World Bank and benefited from diplomatic pressure, succeeded in defusing the situation. But the experience had been traumatic for those involved and the financial returns had fallen well short of what had been expected.

Pakistan ranks poorly on international 'corruption' measures. But this was a very high profile project, launched with strong political support both inside and outside Pakistan. It met an obvious local need. But these factors were clearly insufficient to save the Hubco project from grief.

The Hubco story is not unique. There is a long history of curious political or legal developments which have frustrated investors in Bangkok's rapid transit system, Taiwan's high-speed rail development and electricity developments in India, Indonesia and elsewhere.

In the West it is expected that, in general, laws will not be biased against foreign companies and that they will be impartially interpreted and enforced. Cultural norms elsewhere may be different. An individual in power may be expected to use their position to benefit their relations and friends. Public salaries may be so low that public servants need to accumulate 'extras' to survive. The arrival of Westerners in well-paid, powerful positions may be resented.

Indeed, hostility or resistance to incoming international investment should not be seen as a purely third-world phenomenon. When Henry Ford sought to export his manufacturing revolution to the UK his methods were successfully resisted by British craft-workers who expected to set their own pace and to choose their own working methods. There were sad consequences for the efficiency of the British car industry.

In 1999, José Bové wrecked a McDonald's restaurant under construction in southern France. For what would be considered as an act of vandalism, he was feted as a national hero and invited to dinner by the French prime minister.

It is also worth remembering the insights of F.A. von Hayek's book *The Road to Serfdom*. Where a government takes on the task of directing an economy and involving itself in the huge number of detailed decisions that have to be made, then it will be impossible to subject these decisions to genuine democratic control and impossible to establish detailed legal review. Decisions will have to be arbitrary and unaccountable. And under these circumstances it would be a miracle if corruption did not come to permeate the system. Against this rather sobering background we need to consider some practical aspects of investment in developing economies.

Ownership

Companies will normally assume 100 per cent ownership of projects in developed countries. In developing economies they may accept less – either because local legislation prohibits full foreign ownership or because a local partner seems appropriate to cope with the business environment. Use of locally sourced debt is one method of limiting the downside risk, and a well-connected local partner may be able to arrange this without the need for a parent company guarantee.

The appraisal can either use:

- the project cash flows – although not all of them belong to the foreign investor

- the forecast cash flows from and to the foreign investor; this will involve considering how much can be repatriated over the life of the project.

This second definition of cash flow is more conservative. It tends to make the project look less attractive. However, the more difficult the business environment, the more appropriate it will be.

Currency

Many developing countries have currency controls. These may create difficulty in repatriating profits. As part of the original negotiations it is usual to establish with the local authorities exactly how the rules will be applied. However, countries impose exchange controls because they find it difficult to meet the demand for foreign exchange. Such an imbalance between supply and demand suggests that the local currency may be overvalued. Since it is difficult to sustain an overvalued exchange rate indefinitely, exchange controls may be a sign that the local currency is likely to be devalued. This likelihood would need to be factored into the project appraisal.

Exchange control regimes tend to be modified fairly frequently. Understanding the regime at the time the investment is made may not be sufficient. It is necessary to consider how it might change. In some cases, the signs may be positive and the prospects may be good that controls will be alleviated or abolished. Such signs would include a favourable balance on current account, a sustainable balance on capital account and a black market exchange rate that is close to the official level. Where the signs are strongly negative, it may be advisable to postpone the investment. It is poor management to make a substantial outlay in a developing country just before its currency devalues.

Currency restrictions are another factor that would encourage managers to base the appraisal on forecast cash flows to and from the parent. This would give no weight to currency balances that may be 'blocked' by the exchange regime. In Africa, in particular, international companies have generated local funds which they can neither repatriate nor employ usefully on other projects. The stock market has attached little value to these assets. In China, however, it would appear that some international companies have been so attracted by the long-term prospects – the 'real options' that they perceive from establishing a presence in China – that they have been prepared to overlook the current inconvertibility of the Chinese currency. It is important to note that it is generally impossible to hedge currency exposure in developing economies.

Required returns

First, remember that the basic NPV calculation will be based on expected cash flows – not cash flows assuming that the project proceeds smoothly. In developing countries the difference between these measures may be large, and this is an important way in which risk is incorporated into the analysis.

Otherwise the required return will be set in the same way in developing as in developed countries. The projects may be risky, but most of the additional risk will be specific risk which does not affect required return. A premium for an initial venture in a new business area can be added – just as it would be for domestic projects.

However, these rules apply if the cash flows are being measured at the project level. If the decision has been made to measure parent company cash flows, then additional analysis is required. These cash flows may be highly risky – especially if substantial local debt has been used in the project financing – and need to be discounted at an appropriate rate. The calculation is illustrated in an example.

Example

Red Dot plc is setting up a cement plant in Azaria. It is taking a 50 per cent shareholding (with management control) in the new venture. A prominent local industrial group will hold the remaining 50 per cent. The new venture has arranged a loan facility of 100m Azarian Rupees at 13 per cent interest. Red Dot and its partner are each investing 40m ARs for their equity stakes. The corporate tax rate in Azaria and the UK is 30 per cent.

In the UK Red Dot is much less highly geared. It has calculated its 'Asset β' to be 0.90, which, using CAPM and a risk-free rate of 7 per cent, converts into a required return of 12.9 per cent.

What required return should Red Dot apply to the forecast parent-company cash flows from the Azaria project?

Solution

We use the adjusted present value approach, which is best suited to this type of problem. The required return for the project cash flows (in ARs) might be set at

	12.9%	basic UK rate for current operations
+	4.0%	for a new venture in a risky new business area
+	6.0%	to reflect the higher risk-free rate in Azaria (presumably associated with an inflation rate that is roughly 6 per cent higher than the UK)
	22.9%	

This is the 'project' rate. We can calculate that this corresponds to an 'Asset B' of 1.52, since, using the CAPM formula

$$22.9\% = 13\% + (\beta_A \times 6.5\%)$$

$$\beta_A = 1.52.$$

We now calculate the β for the equity cash flows to Red Dot in the UK. We know from Chapter 3 that

$$\beta_A = \frac{E}{E + D(1 - T)} \cdot \beta_E$$

Applying the Azarian project numbers, this gives

$$1.52 = \frac{80M}{80M + 100M(1 - 0.30)} \cdot \beta_E$$

hence $\beta_E = 2.85$

and the required return for the 'equity' cash flows back to the parent company, again using CAPM, is

$$13\% + (2.85 \times 6.5\%) = 31.5\%.$$

The rate looks extremely high. This is partly because the cash flows are being measured in ARs, where the risk-free rate is 13 per cent. Also, Azaria has higher inflation than the UK and this inflation will have a positive effect on the forecast cash flows. However, the rate is also high because the project has a large 'prior charge' in terms of the commitment to repay the loan. This has geared up the returns to the UK parent company and the high required return reflects this fact.

Summary of international investment appraisal

International investment, especially in developing economies, occupies the turbulent zone where Western capital meets non-Western cultures. Our discussion has emphasised the difficulties that can arise. Certainly international companies need to enter these markets with their eyes open to the problems that may arise. But there are many stories of companies that have found the formula for success. BAT has a highly successful, market-leading cigarette business in Brazil. It is well accepted in the local environment. Since it collects excise taxes it is, by one measure, the largest taxpayer in the country. HSBC has a very successful banking business in the Far East. Bae Systems has a major, long-term contract with Saudi Arabia which provides an important part of its business. Coca-Cola has successfully developed a global brand – and finds that most of its new customers have been in developing markets. There are very large opportunities available but they need to be approached with caution.

REPLACEMENT AND TIMING

There is a set of specialised techniques for choosing the optimal time to replace an asset, the optimal time to introduce a new type of asset and the best way to chose between alternative assets with different lives. In all of the following examples we shall assume that the company plans to sell its product or service indefinitely. The underlying 'project' is permanent. To sustain this business a sequence of assets is employed, each item being replaced when a new asset, the 'challenger', shows that it can do the job more cost effectively.

All these techniques involve the calculation of an 'annual cost' or 'annualised cost' of an asset. We shall start by demonstrating their calculation.

Annual Cost and Annualised Cost

The annual cost of owning and operating an asset is the sum of money, X, defined as follows:

Proceeds from selling the asset at the beginning of the year =

$$\frac{\text{Proceeds from selling the asset at the end of the year } - \text{ Maintenance Expenditure } + X}{1 + k}$$

where k is the appropriate interest rate. The annual cost relates to a single year. It will vary from year to year during the asset's life.

An annualised cost, Y, covers a number of years, N.

It is defined so that an annual payment of Y, made at the end of each of the N years, has the same present value as: 'Acquisition cost at the beginning of the period + The present value of the maintenance costs during the period – The present value of the proceeds of disposal at the end of the period.'

Exactly what costs should be included in 'maintenance' will vary with the context. Costs that are the same for the alternatives under consideration can be excluded. Other costs should be included in the analysis.

Example

Consider an airline which is deciding how long to keep its jet engines. The value of an engine after N years, and the annual maintenance costs (which will, of course, include the opportunity cost of having aircraft out of service) are given in columns two and three. From these numbers, the annual cost of engine ownership, and the annualized costs for different lives are calculated. The appropriate interest rate is 10 per cent

(1)	(2)	(3)	(4)	(5)
Year	Engine value	Maintenance	Annual cost	Annualised cost
	(£'000)	(£'000)	(£'000)	(£'000)
0	1,200			
1	970	50	400	400
2	810	120	377	389
3	690	170	371	384
4	600	220	379	383
5	520	260	400	385
6	450	310	432	391

We can check the derivation of these numbers. The annual cost of ownership for the third year (£371,000) is calculated from

X = (Beginning of year value)$(1 + k)$ − (End of year value) + (Maintenance for year)

$$= 810(1.1) - 690 + 170$$

$$= 371$$

To calculate the annualized cost over a three-year ownership period, we set the present value of three equal annual payments

$$\frac{Y}{1.1} + \frac{Y}{(1.1)^2} + \frac{Y}{(1.1)^3}$$

equal to the present value of buying, maintaining and subsequently selling an engine over a three-year period.

$$1{,}200 - \frac{50}{1.1} - \frac{120}{(1.1)^2} - \frac{170}{(1.1)^3} + \frac{690}{(1.1)^3}$$

Solving this gives Y = 384

Note that the annual costs and the annualised costs are closely related. The present value of the annual costs over the first three years

$$\frac{400}{1.1} + \frac{377}{(1.1)^2} + \frac{371}{(1.1)^3} = 954$$

is equal to the present value of the annualised cost over the period

$$\frac{384}{1.1} + \frac{384}{(1.1)^2} + \frac{384}{(1.1)^3} = 954$$

The annualised cost is simply a way of expressing the total cost over a period as an equal annual amount.

The numbers can be shown graphically (Figure 7.1).

The relationship between annual and annualised costs is very similar to the relationship between marginal cost and average cost in standard economic analysis. In principal, the annual cost curve will go through the lowest point of the annualised cost line, although this may be hard to observe, since we only have a few discrete points available.

Fig. 7.1

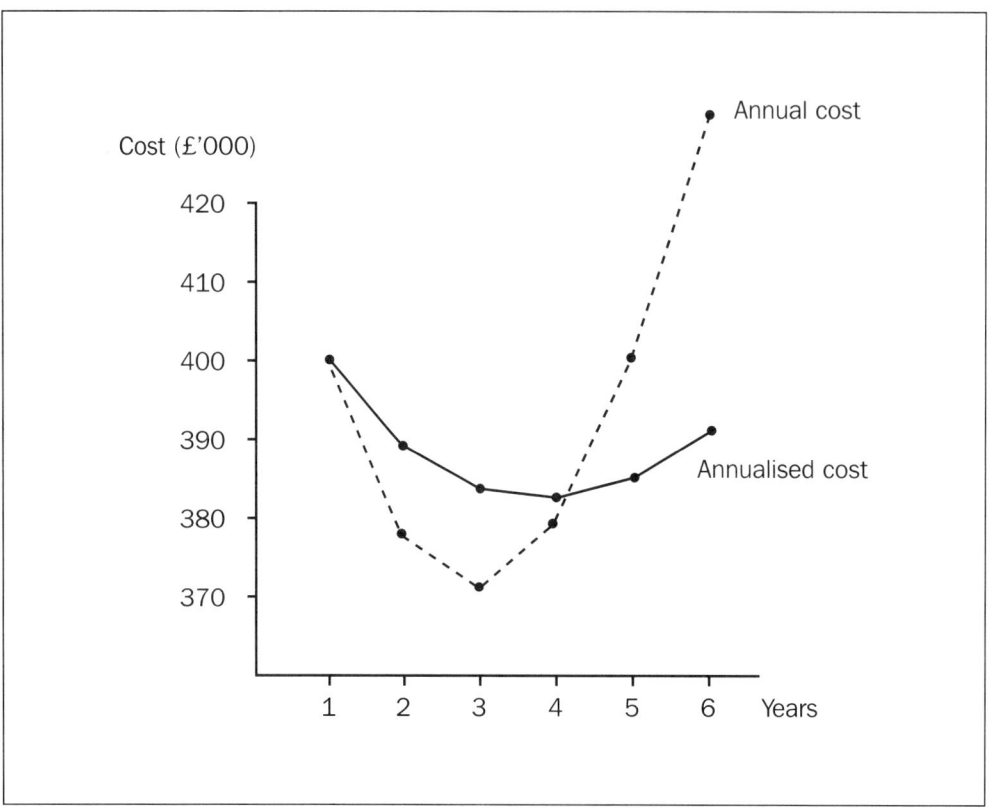

With sophisticated financial markets, a company purchasing a capital asset may well be asked whether it would like to pay a lump sum or make a series of 'rent', 'hire purchase' or 'lease' payments. Annualised cost is sometimes called 'equivalent annual rental'. However, the validity of the technique does not depend on the financing method used, and decisions can be based on an annualised cost calculation even if the asset will be purchased for cash.

The optimal life

If we buy a new engine, how long should we keep it? Answer – we should replace it on a cycle which gives us the lowest annualised ownership cost. In this case, four years. Notice that the annualised cost curve is very flat. £384 for a three-year cycle; £383 for four years; £385 for five years. It is generally true that curves will be pretty flat at the bottom, but there is a further explanation for this phenomenon. The prices of second-hand engines will tend to adjust to equalise the annual costs of ownership in different years. If all engine-using companies had exactly the same cost structures, then we would expect that both the annual cost curve and the annualised cost curve would be flat – up to the point where the engine ends its useful life and is sold off as scrap.

We have assumed that the jet engine will be bought new. If we did not impose this condition, the cheapest way for the airline to operate would be to buy two-year-old engines and sell them after a year. This gives an annual cost of only £371. However, second-hand equipment is often a difficult and illiquid market, and this is likely to be an impractical policy.

Choosing between assets

There may be several jet-engine manufacturers, whose products differ in numerous subtle ways. Which one to choose? Again, the annualised cost method solves the problem. The optimal choice is the one which offers the lowest annualised cost. This may not be the engine which is the cheapest to buy, or the engine which has the longest life, or the engine which has the lowest maintenance costs. The annualised cost method takes all these factors into account simultaneously.

This is a technique with wide application. It can be used to choose road surfaces for public authorities; for the choice between petrol or diesel cars for fleet managers or to decide between wooden and PVC window frames for those planning new buildings.

Replacing an existing asset with a newly available dissimilar asset

The implicit assumption in the basic annualised cost method is that when the current asset is discarded it will be replaced by another identical item. We can compare the annualised cost for, say, a four-year life-cycle petrol truck with a six-year life-cycle diesel truck because, in both cases, the annualised cost that we calculate is a cost in perpetuity. We make four notional annual payments for the first petrol truck, but then we can acquire a replacement truck and pay for it by continuing the same series of notional annual payments.

Sometimes a new asset – the 'challenger' – becomes available, which will do the same job as the 'defender' but has a new set of financial figures. How do we decide whether the change should be made? And how do we decide whether the change should be made immediately or after some delay? One possibility is when the 'defender' was already scheduled for replacement.

Again, the solution is annualised cost. Treat the 'defender' as if it were a new asset which was being purchased today at its disposal value. Calculate the annualised cost if you keep the defender for one, two or three years.

Then calculate the annualised cost (over an optimal life-span) for the challenger. If this cost is lower than the annualised cost of the defender (over all possible remaining life spans), then the challenger wins outright and the defender should be sold immediately.

If not, the defender has a stay of execution. Look at the annual (not annualised) costs of continuing to own it. We shall assume that these are either monotonically increasing (so the machine gets more expensive to own and operate as it gets older) or are U-shaped (as in the jet engine example in Figure 7.1). Sell the defender just before its *annual* cost rises above the *annualised* cost of the challenger. This situation is pictured in Figure 7.2. The diagram illustrates a situation in which the defender should be retained for two more years, and then replaced by the challenger.

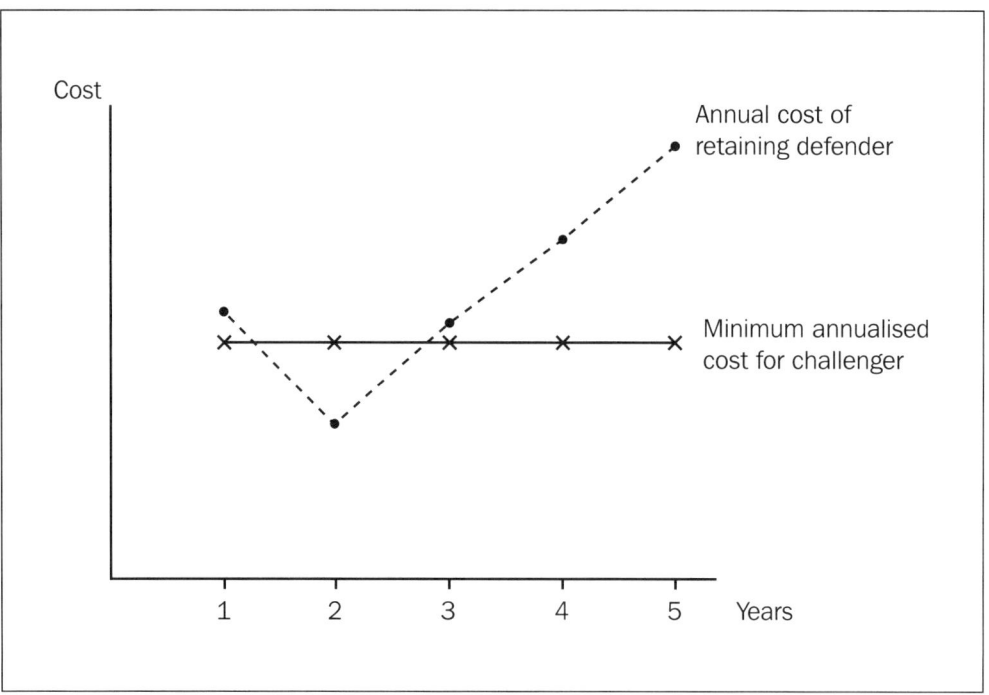

Fig. 7.2

Inflation

The assumption behind annualised cost calculations is that a new asset can be purchased at the same price as the one that it replaces. In an inflationary environment, this will not be a credible assumption. However, if we assume that all prices will rise in line with overall inflation – and we are prepared to make an estimate of future inflation – then the calculations can easily be adapted. Instead of calculating an annualised cost that is constant in money terms, we calculate an annual cost that is constant in purchasing power terms. In money terms, it will rise each year at the rate of inflation.

In the jet-engine example, we calculated the annualised cost over a three-year life to be 384. Let us recalculate this figure, assuming inflation of 6 per cent. We further assume that the maintenance costs and disposal value are at current prices and will be affected by inflation. A three-year-old engine that is sold today will fetch £690 – as in the table. If such an engine is sold in three years' time, however, it will fetch

$$690(1.06)^3 = 822$$

Our annual cost, Y, is an amount that will rise at 6% per year. The present value is

$$\frac{Y(1.06)}{1.10} + \frac{Y(1.06)^2}{(1.10)^2} + \frac{Y(1.06)^3}{(1.10)^3}$$

and we set this equal to

$$-1,200 - \frac{50(1.06)}{(1.1)} - \frac{120(1.06)^2}{(1.1)^2} - \frac{170(1.06)^3}{(1.1)^3} + \frac{690(1.06)^3}{(1.1)^3}$$

which gives Y = 321.

The engine could be purchased, maintained and sold over a three-year cycle for annual payments of

1st year	321
2nd year	$321(1.06) = 340.3$
3rd year	$321(1.06)^2 = 360.7$

Each of these three payments would have the same purchasing power. And a replacement jet engine could be obtained for the following three years by continuing the series of payments.

4th year	$321(1.06)^4 = 405.3$
5th year	$321(1.06)^5 = 429.6$
6th year	$321(1.06)^6 = 455.3$

We simply record the three-year annualised cost as 321 and use this number as before. The optimum life for the asset is the one that gives the lowest 'constant purchasing power' annualised cost.

Notice that, in this calculation, future payments are being inflated by an annual factor 1.06, and are also being discounted by a factor 1.10. It is possible to integrate these two elements. Since

$$\frac{1.06}{1.10} = \frac{1}{1.0377}$$

the annualised cost could have been calculated directly using a discount rate of 3.77%. What is 3.77%? It is the real rate of interest in this situation, as explained in chapter 3 (see page 39).

So this section can be simply summarised. In an inflationary environment, calculate annual and annualised costs using the 'real' rather than the 'nominal' interest rate. But note that annual and annualised cost calculated from one base date cannot be directly compared with costs calculated from another.

Advancing technology

We now return to zero inflation and consider another possibility. Suppose that assets are becoming cheaper every year as technology improves. We shall switch to calling assets computers (rather than jet engines) to make the example more realistic, but we shall use the same basic numbers. Suppose that the improvement factor is 5 per cent per year.

This situation has some similarity to the inflation problem. The series of annual payments that will keep the company supplied with computers in perpetuity, is a series that will fall by a factor of 0.95 each year. The difference, compared to the inflation situation, is that we shall assume that technological advance does not reduce the maintenance costs of existing machines. But we shall assume that the disposal value of old machines is affected. A computer bought today and sold after three years will therefore realise only

$$690(0.95)^3 = 592$$

The annualised cost number for a three-year life cycle is therefore calculated by setting

$$\frac{Y}{(1.10)} + \frac{Y(0.95)}{(1.10)^2} + \frac{Y(0.95)^2}{(1.10)^3}$$

$$-1{,}200 - \frac{50}{(1.10)} - \frac{120}{(1.10)^2} - \frac{170}{(1.10)^3} + \frac{690(0.95)^3}{(1.10)^3}$$

which gives Y = 450.

The company can supply itself with computers in perpetuity in exchange for a series of annual payments.

450; 427.5; 406; (new computer) 386; 367; 348; (new computer) 331; etc.

As long as we ensure that the 'base dates' from which they have been made are compatible, these numbers can be used to decide between competing models; to decide how long to keep a computer before it becomes obsolete and, when faced with an unexpected jump in technology, whether to give an installed computer 'early retirement' and replace it with next generation equipment.

Replacement and life-cycle decisions with limited data

As the preceding sections have shown, there is a full set of techniques available for optimising replacement decisions. The limiting factor in using them is the availability of data. Even if there is limited information available, it is usually possible to do a rough calculation. What is the annual cost of holding on to the defender for one more year? What is the annualised cost of the challenger? The time to change is when next year's annual cost (defender) looks as though it will exceed the challenger's annualised cost.

LEASING

Leasing is an alternative to ownership for companies seeking to acquire the use of an asset. It is used on a large scale in the UK and elsewhere. In this section we shall see how to compare the attractiveness of these two methods.

Leases are sometimes divided into 'financial' leases and 'service' (sometimes 'operating') leases. A service lease is usually arranged between the user of an asset and a manufacturer. In return for the lease payments, the user will get the asset along with service and maintenance, compensation for any failure of the asset to perform as promised and, perhaps, a second-hand price guarantee if the user wants to dispose of the asset or trade up to more modern equipment.

Leases of this type are increasingly common for airframe manufacturers, jet-engine builders, car manufacturers, train-set constructors, etc. They recognise that, logically, the manufacturer should take responsibility for their product. However, the analysis of this type of lease is complicated because of the need to place a value on the various different parts of the package.

Financial leases are more straightforward. The counterpart is usually a finance house which is a subsidiary of a bank. There are no additional features in the contract beyond the supply of the asset. And the deal is generally a 'full payout' lease in which the user agrees irrevocably (or nearly irrevocably, for reasons we shall soon discuss) to make a series of lease payments that will cover the full cash price of the asset. So long as the user is creditworthy, there is no prospect that the asset will be returned early. And assessing creditworthiness, of course, is a banker's core skill. The involvement of the bank is purely financial.

The commitment for a company with a financial lease is very similar to the obligation under a 'borrow-and-buy' policy. It is these alternatives which are commonly compared.

Leasing and tax

The essential characteristic of leasing from a financial analysis point of view is that it qualifies for special tax treatment. If an asset is purchased, the company will get writing-down allowances. If it borrows the money the interest payments will be deductible. If it leases, the lease payments will be tax deductible (and the writing-down allowances will go to the finance house which, technically, owns the asset).

This tax system makes leasing attractive to companies which are not paying corporate tax. This might be because business is poor – but it might also be because they are new businesses with considerable start-up expenses in relation to revenue. Such companies could not make use of writing down allowances – they have no tax bill to cut. They have no 'tax capacity'. However, by leasing an asset they can put the writing-down allowances into the hands of the finance house which will have 'tax capacity'. Non-taxpaying entities such as charities can find leasing attractive for the same reason.

The difference in tax treatment was historically matched by a difference in accounting treatment. A purchased asset appeared on the balance sheet, as did any debt used to buy it. A leased asset, not 'owned' by the company, did not appear as an asset and the commitment to make lease payments did not appear as a liability. Any disclosure would appear elsewhere, in notes to the accounts.

This was anomalous and intellectually indefensible. The accounting bodies in the UK and elsewhere have established a set of rules to identify leases which are deemed equivalent to ownership. For such leases, the asset and the associated liability are to be shown directly in the balance sheet. And the Inland Revenue has decided that what is logical for accounting purposes is also logical for their purposes. Such leases will be treated for tax purposes as if their legal form had been borrow-and-buy.

However, this treatment is highly unpopular with finance directors. More assets and liabilities on the balance sheet tend to hurt their financial ratios. Nor do they like losing tax breaks. A great deal of ingenuity has been used, therefore, to design lease agreements that just escape being caught by the new rules. One example is aircraft operated by a well-known British airline. While they were very visible at airports, they were much less so in the company accounts. In this section we shall analyse leases that have qualified for the 'traditional' tax treatment.

The NPV of a lease

The lease NPV will be the present value of the stream of after-tax cash flows associated with obtaining the use of the asset. The NPV of borrow-and-buy will be defined in the equivalent way. Note that all the cash flows will be near certain. The company must make the lease or debt payments if it is to continue in business. It will get the tax benefits so long as it retains tax capacity. There is some risk associated with changing corporate tax rates (and lease agreements normally specify that this risk is born by the lessee) but this risk is comparatively minor. We do not, therefore, face the problem of deriving a risk-adjusted rate. All the calculations are normally done at the company's best borrowing rate.

Example

Boyce Airways is considering whether to buy or lease a new aircraft. Boyce pays corporate tax at a rate of 30 per cent and is a highly creditworthy company with a borrowing rate of 9 per cent. Tax is paid with a one-year lag. It expects to dispose of the aircraft after a life of seven years. The alternatives are as follows.

- Buy the aircraft for £1.8m cash. Borrow this amount, making an annual repayment of £357,600 at the end of each of the seven years. Boyce can claim a writing-down allowance of 25 per cent of the declining balance. At the end of year seven, it is expected that the aircraft can be sold for £400,000.

- Lease the aircraft for £304,000 per year, payable at the beginning of each year. At the end of seven years, Boyce agrees to reimburse the tax finance house for the difference between £400,000 and the market value of seven-year-old aircraft. (This makes the lease strictly comparable with the purchase. Boyce will benefit if second hand aircraft values exceed expectations, and will suffer if they are lower.)

The NPV of the lease payments is calculated from the cash flows (£'000)

Year 0	Year 1	Year 2	Year 3	Year 4	Year 5	Year 6	Year 7	Year 8
(304)	(304)	(304)	(304)	(304)	(304)	(304)		
	91.2	91.2	91.2	91.2	91.2	91.2	91.2	
(304)	(212.8)	(212.8)	(212.8)	(212.8)	(212.8)	(212.8)	91.2	

and the NPV of these payments at 9 per cent is (1,209).

If the asset is purchased, the company benefits from the writing-down allowances and the tax deductibility of interest. The interest component of the debt repayment can be readily calculated. Having borrowed £1.8m, the interest due in the first year is 9 per cent of this, £162,000. The annual payment is £357,600 and, if £162,000 goes in interest in the first year, the remaining £195,600 is available to reduce the outstanding debt. Year two, therefore, starts with a debt of £1.6044m and interest for year two is £144,400. This method gives the interest component for each year.

	Year 0	Year 1	Year 2	Year3	Year 4	Year 5	Year 6	Year 7	Year 8
Purchase price	−1,800							400	
Loan	1,800	−357.6	−357.6	−357.6	−357.6	−357.6	−357.6	−357.6	
Interest (tax deductible)		162.0	144.4	125.2	104.3	81.5	56.6	29.5	
WDA (tax deductible)		450.0	337.5	253.1	189.8	42.4	106.8	80.1	
Write-off on disposal (tax deductible)								240.3	
Tax at 30%			183.6	144.6	113.5	88.2	67.2	49.0	−15.0
Net cash flow		−357.6	−174.0	−213.0	−244.1	−269.4	−290.4	91.4	−15.0

The NPV of these net cash flows at 9 per cent is −1,118. Both the NPVs are negative reflecting the cost of the aircraft. The borrow-and-buy cash flows give the smaller cost, so this is the preferred alternative.

Partial debt replacement

We have assumed that if the asset is not leased, the whole price of the asset will be financed with debt. It is true that these methods involve broadly similar financial obligations, so that they appear to be natural alternatives. However, one of the advantages of leasing is that it can stretch the borrowing power of companies that are close to their limit. Let us consider a case in which the alternative to a lease is 30 per cent debt; 70 per cent equity.

When equity is used to substitute for debt in this way, no additional risk is created. (Nearly) risk-free debt is replaced by (nearly) risk-free equity. So the cost of equity would, in our example, still be 9 per cent. The only difference would be that there would be no interest payments and therefore no tax deductions associated with the equity.

In the Boyce Airways example above, the present value of the tax subsidies to interest payments are £149,600. If the aircraft was financed 30 per cent by debt, the value of the tax subsidies would become £149,600 × 0.30 = £44,880, and the NPV of borrow-and-buy would fall by £104,720 to £−1,233,000. This would tip the balance. One hundred per cent debt beats leasing; but leasing beats a 30 per cent debt/70 per cent equity financing package.

The accuracy of lease calculations

In many areas of investment appraisal we have elegant mathematical techniques but find it difficult to get accurate data in order to use them. This is not the case for lease calculations. Because we are considering financial policy the numbers for both alternatives will generally be known with great accuracy. This can be reflected in the financial analysis. It is often appropriate to consider the lease alternative when acquiring assets. The deal can often still be structured to gain tax advantages and avoid pressure on the balance sheet. Studies have shown that leasing is a highly competitive market. Lessees can get the benefit, indirectly, of the writing-down allowances which they generate for the lessors.

CONCLUSIONS

This chapter has considered a range of specialised appraisal techniques. Asset replacement decisions and life-cycle decisions require the calculation of annual costs and annualised costs. Once these concepts are understood, the logic behind those decisions becomes clear and the calculations themselves should not present difficulty.

The chapter also considered the analysis of leases – in particular, leases which qualify for 'traditional' tax treatment. There are no new principles involved in lease analysis. The after-tax cash flows from the two financing alternatives are compared. Leasing is an important method by which companies acquire assets, and a detailed analysis of this particular financing technique has therefore been provided.

8

Conclusions

GENERAL SUMMARY

The central theme of this briefing has been the close relationship between the NPV of a company's projects and the value created for shareholders. No other evaluation method can match NPV in this respect. IRR or payback can be very misleading. Measures based on profit are fundamentally flawed. The fact that a project will generate a profit does not imply that it is attractive to shareholders. Profit measures do not attempt to answer the key question: 'Does this project cover the opportunity cost of the capital employed?'

The briefing has explained and illustrated the techniques for measuring NPV and shareholder value. It has covered the following in detail.

- *The identification of cash flows that should be included in the analysis.* In principle, all incremental cash flows which will impact on shareholder wealth should be included. These flows can be difficult to identify and to quantify. The text discussed how such difficulties might be resolved.

- *The measurement of the required return – the opportunity cost of the capital employed on a project.* The briefing argued that required returns were risk-related and showed several ways in which this logic could be applied. A single required return may be established for the whole company; different returns may be established for different divisions depending on the nature of their business; or returns may be tailored to the characteristics of individual projects. The choice will depend on the level of detail and complexity that is deemed appropriate. Large projects justify a more sophisticated analysis than small ones.

- *NPV methods.* The WACC method was simple and highly practical in divisionalised companies. APV is more accurate in its treatment of interest tax subsidies but is more complex. Once again, there is a trade-off between simplicity and accuracy.

- *Risk analysis.* This briefing has recommended that projects should be subject to risk analysis, and has explained how to employ these techniques. Risk analysis adds value by:
  - identifying the main contributors to project risk; the company can then consider if and how these risk elements could be reduced
  - improving the accuracy of the NPV calculation, recognising that risk may not be symmetrical on the upside and the downside.
  - evaluating the possibility that the project may fail so seriously that it prevents the company from taking up valuable growth opportunities.

The briefing also recommends that companies should try to identify and evaluate the real options that may be created or destroyed by accepting a project.

- *Replacement decisions*. The optimisation of asset replacement and life-cycle decisions. The techniques used in this specialised area of project appraisal were explained and illustrated.

- *Other appraisal techniques*. The text also explained the particular appraisal techniques associated with international investment and the use of lease finance.

THEMES

Project appraisal is widely taught in universities and business schools, and it appears in the syllabus for many professional examinations. This has been both an advantage and a disadvantage. The subject has gained in rigour from academic involvement. But a disadvantage is that many managers first meet project appraisal in the context of carefully constructed examination questions where all data are neatly supplied, all consequences are easily quantifiable and the problem has been carefully bounded to exclude indirect and 'knock-on' effects on the company's business.

This briefing recognises that appraisal in practice is very different from the idealised appraisal of the examination hall. It has not attempted to include mathematical techniques – for example linear programming or dynamic optimisation – for which data is very rarely available in the real world.

Putting project appraisal techniques into practice is very often a matter of rough estimation and broad simplification. The objective is to be *roughly right* rather than *precisely wrong*. Appraisal should attempt to include all the consequences of a project that will impact on shareholders. This will often include prospects that can only be vaguely outlined at the time of the decision. Project appraisal should not be based on principles of prudence or conservatism. The object is to include and quantify, if at all possible, even the indirect and uncertain consequences. The appraiser should not be reluctant to show imagination and creativity in this aspect of his/her job.

One accounting principle that is relevant in an appraisal context is materiality. It is not always beneficial to track down, for example, every tax implication of asset disposal at the end of a project's life. Where the numbers are small in relation to the scale of the investment, a simplified treatment can be justified. Good projects will clearly show themselves as good; bad projects will stand out as bad. As for marginal projects, where the decision might be tipped by a small item, their marginality means that the decision one way or the other will make little difference.

We saw at the beginning of this briefing that a large component of stock-market value relates to 'growth opportunities'. These are options to undertake investment projects in the future. If investment appraisal is to focus on shareholders' value, therefore, it must give a prominent role to this part of the process. Any company which regards itself as a growth business, and believes that its shares deserve a high price/earnings multiple, must expect real options to play a major part in the appraisal of its larger and more strategic projects. The difficulty of evaluating these options is not an acceptable excuse. In some cases it may be possible to visualise the new project as a stand-alone business and to value it with reference to comparable quoted businesses. Formal option evaluation models, designed for financial options, may be helpful, although real options have rather different characteristics. Broad estimates of option value may be the best achievable, but they should still be included in the calculations. The key assumptions should be made clear to encourage constructive management debate.

Many investments are directed towards intangible outcomes such as quality improvement or better customer service. It is important to try and relate these gains to shareholder value. It is a challenge to management to develop a sufficiently sophisticated model of customer behaviour in their industry that these types of benefits can be valued. To invest in 'improved service' with no conceptual link between this factor and incremental sales or higher retention rates is difficult to justify. Project appraisal may well require an associated investment in market research or model development.

A good investment is not necessarily one that silences all argument at the executive committee. It should bring out clearly the key assumptions on which the valuation rests and the basis or source of these assumptions. Some of these are likely to be factual and non-controversial. Others may be more subjective. It can be very beneficial if appraisal stimulates an argument and brings in a wider group of experienced managers to contribute constructively to the evaluation process.

This would counteract one common criticism of appraisal practice – that appraisal is a technical chore to be performed after the key decisions have been made at a higher level. In such a system, appraisal obviously adds no value. To be useful, appraisal must precede and inform the key decision-making events.

APPRAISAL REPORTS

An appraisal report should include the spreadsheet on which the basic NPV calculation is based. It should also include information from the risk analysis; information on real options associated with the project; information on alternative ways in which the opportunity might be exploited; information on the source of the data from which the NPV has been derived. This information will give a more complete picture of the project and will provide a basis for productive debate.

Illustration

An illustration of this approach, a report on the Modern Ceramics project, discussed in Chapter 6, is set out below. The spreadsheets and diagrams, as discussed in the text, are not included here, but should be attached as part of the overall report.

Investment Approval Request AA.01/00

Project Title Hawkney Signed Plates

Project Description In accordance with a draft agreement (attached) with Derek Hawkney and his gallery, Modern Ceramics would manufacture and paint 800 plates to Hawkney designs. These would be signed by Mr Hawkney and sold through art galleries, primarily in the US but with significant sales in the UK.

Alternatives considered

1. Manufacture of plates by Modern Ceramics with marketing and distribution by a third party has been investigated. Analysis has suggested that this is an unattractive alternative, due to the high mark-up that would be required and the inability of such a marketing company to add value.

2. Linking with an artist other than Hawkney. While some other artists might be suitable partners, Hawkney is our clear first choice on the basis of artistic reputation, public popularity and the suitability of his artistic output for this purpose.

Risk category

This is a new venture for Modern Ceramics and is innovative in industry terms. The required return is therefore set at 15.0 per cent.

Initial Outlay	–	Expected to be £213,750
Project Duration	–	Project expected to be completed after three years.
		May last longer if sales are slower than expected. By contract with Mr Hawkney, project must end after five years.
Cash Flow Schedules	–	Attached.
NPV	–	£34,037 (but see 'Risk analysis' below).

Key risk factors and sources of information

1. Rate of sales – marketing director, advised by Mr Hawkney's gallery, has contacted 11 potential outlets – 3 in California, 5 in other parts of the US, 3 in Europe. All responded positively. Sales estimates based, conservatively, on their prediction.

2. Exchange rates – based on the historic volatility of the £/$ rate.

3. Scrappage – based on experience in producing items to the specification of leading potters.

Risk analysis

Sensitivity Analysis identified the sales rate as the major risk factor. There was also exchange rate risk. Simulation showed that the project had greater downside than upside potential and that the mean NPV was £5,255.

In the light of this analysis we have:

- negotiated an exit route whereby plates can be sold to leading hotel chains if the original marketing plan fails. This has raised the mean simulated NPV to £16,061

- reduced currency exposure by agreeing the annual level of marketing support in dollars rather than pounds.

This project is very unlikely to have an adverse effect on the development of the rest of the company's business.

Options

Four other leading artists have been identified as suitable partners for Modern Ceramics. Their galleries are interested, and we have agreed to inform them of the progress of the Hawkney set. If this project is successful, we could expect to sell 2,000 plates within seven years. These copycat projects would be less risky than the current path-breaking development. We estimate a 50 per cent chance that follow-on projects will be launched, with an NPV of £40,000 based on the Hawkney precedent. The value of the options associated with this project are very roughly estimated at £20,000.

The project would not destroy any of our current options. Production of the Hawkney plates can be accommodated as an addition to other production plans. There is no opportunity cost in terms of other projects forgone.

CONCLUSION

The development of discounted cash flow techniques has been an enormous advance in the technique of project appraisal. Over the past 30 years it has spread into the management process of almost all major companies. Subsequent developments have not undermined the logic of NPV.

However, the emphasis on NPV has had some negative effects. It has encouraged a focus on hard, 'guaranteed' numbers rather than a broader, but perhaps less accurate, assessment of a project's implications. This, in turn, may have produced a bias towards cost reduction projects (where outcomes are often fairly predictable) rather than corporate expansion (where they are not).

One objective of this briefing has been to redress this balance and to take a broader, longer-term look at the creation of shareholder value. It recommends appraisals using estimates which are 'best guesses' not conservative minima, which use risk analysis to identify and to control by management action the upside and downside potentials; and which incorporate an analysis of the real options embedded in the project, options that we know to be a major component of shareholder value.